STE

OUT ON THE PROMISE

From Vision to Reality

A journey towards excellent education in a Christian context

TITILAYO OLUWATUDIMU

Book cover design and illustration
by Andy Colthart JHarts Design and Print
http://www.jharts.co.uk/

Edited and Published by The Heritage Publishers
www.theheritagepublishers.com

First Printed in the United Kingdom in 2022
by Oluwatudimu, Titilayo

Emmanuel Community School Website:
https://www.emmanuelcommunityschool.co.uk/

The Emmanuel School Trust:
https://theemmanuelschooltrust.co.uk/

CONTENTS

"For I know the thoughts that I have toward
you says the Lord, thoughts of peace and not of evil;
to give you a future and a hope."

Jeremiah 29:11 (NKJV)

FOREWORD

How can I ever forget the Sunday morning when Titilayo and her husband Akin tapped me on the shoulder after a morning service in our church and asked if I was aware of the national opportunity being offered for the setting up of Free School Academies? I had to confess that, apart from a few news bulletins and media articles, I had not investigated this issue. They assured me that they had! In fact, beyond a cursory assessment of the matter, they were convinced that this opportunity was something Christian communities should look at seriously and fully engage with. I resonated with this because our church was well populated with educationalists and, at leadership level, we had reflected more than once on why God had configured our congregation in such a way…was it an indication of purpose?

My resonance also had historic roots. The first Sunday Schools were established in England in 1780, to reach out to poor, illiterate children working under brutal conditions in factories. These classes taught basic reading and writing, as well as Biblical principles. Millions of children were reached.

Robert Raikes (1735-1811) is traditionally credited as pioneering Sunday Schools, but wider facts indicate that teaching Bible reading and basic skills on a Sunday was an established activity in a number of eighteenth century Puritan and evangelical congregations. However, the cheerful and energetic Raikes was a significant figure in the growth and development of the Sunday School movement. Additional personalities that aided this were Hannah and Martha Moore, sisters who initiated some real innovation in the delivery of curriculum, projects and community publicity for the schools. They were an inspiration for hub development across the country. Chapels that took onboard the innovation and energy of the Sunday School movement became more inviting – had better music – which was attractive to the young and beneficial to all.

They started sewing classes, bazaars, concerts, drama productions, cricket and football clubs, plus numerous societies for mutual improvement. Add to this the excursions to the seaside, and Sunday School was the place to be! There can be no denying the amazing role the Church played in this great educational movement!

Titilayo became the lead proposer and engine room at the heart of this vision. Add to this a small team of willing volunteers and we were off! To watch things move from dream to design, and then on to delivery, has been a breath-taking, rollercoaster ride but an amazing thing to see! For the first year of the school's operation, it was housed in our church building. The church members supported all manner of school activity, served as staff, governors and maintenance crews! The vision for a community school had come to life before our eyes.

We are now a school with a Christian designation, Ofsted affirmation, and community appreciation. Our Christian platform is not leveraged for proselytism but is firmly committed to a curriculum of full and fair education. However, we are grateful to be anchored to the historic values that have shaped education across this nation.

We invite you to read our story and share the dream!

Pastor Doug Williams BD MTh,

Senior Pastor, Emmanuel Community Church International, Walthamstow.

INTRODUCTION

This brief narrative is about the establishment of Emmanuel Community School, Walthamstow (ECS), the first 'Free School' to open in the London Borough of Waltham Forest. Highlighting aspects of the journey, from the challenges of starting a new collaborative initiative 'from scratch', as they say, to our first cohort of graduates leaving to continue their educational journeys into secondary school, the book covers the seven-year period up till July 2019.

Since then, we have had the pleasure of seeing more children pass through the school to swell the ranks of an increasing group of alumni, who are making a positive impact wherever they go. Over the 10-year journey since September 2012, when the first twenty students were admitted into our temporary premises in Walthamstow, East London, there have been exhilarating moments of great achievements and pride in our students. There were also low points when, as the primary visionary behind this initiative, I despaired about our continued ability to deliver the excellent education we signed up to provide.

Much more could be written about this journey, such as educational achievements and the correlation between student attainments in inner city settings and the socio-economic or demographic context in which the school operates. However, that's for another day. The focus has been to present the reader with a narrative 'as it happens'. Much like, when a parent or grandparent walks a young child to school, the adult needs to allow time for the questions, games and child-like wonderment attached to items adults would not normally pay much attention to.

Much of the information we compiled in sections 2 and 3 of this book had previously been passed on to parents in our weekly newsletters, and in the pictorial yearbooks which commemorate the graduation of our cohorts.

The school's core values are expressed through biblical principles, and the rainbow, with its rich colours and significance as an indication of divine promises, reminds us of the context of our name: Emmanuel, which means God with us.

The reference in Jeremiah 29:11 indicates a declaration and promise from God, delivered to a set of people in exile through the prophet Jeremiah in the Christian Bible. We firmly believe our children are entitled to a bright future and great hope, irrespective of their background, abilities or provenience. The Emmanuel School Trust (TEST) remains committed to our *raison d'etre*, expressed in our school motto – BECAUSE EVERYONE HAS A FUTURE – as coined by Adam Brown, aged about 10 years, in a competition back in 2011.

We are incredibly grateful to the Department for Education and their agencies, such as the Education and Skills Funding Agency (ESFA) and the Regional Schools Commissioner, for entrusting The Emmanuel School Trust with the task of establishing and operating Emmanuel Community School, and for providing public funding.

We would also like to express our deepest gratitude to everyone who has made this journey possible – from our splendid children and alumni to all our parents, grandparents, and guardians, through to our teaching and non-teaching staff, governors, trustees, volunteers, partner churches and so many other stakeholders. I am also grateful to my husband Akin Oluwatudimu, who has worked alongside me in this initiative and helped with editing this book.

Mrs Titilayo Oluwatudimu

PART ONE

BY OUR LEAD PROPOSER – HOW IT ALL BEGAN

1

PREPARATION

It was a pleasant June morning in 2010, on the A406 North Circular Road in London, my usual morning commute to school since I started my Future Leader's residency and role as Deputy headteacher of St. Mary's Church of England School in September 2008. The radio in the little red Fiat Punto was tuned to Radio 1, unlike my usual morning choice of Premier Christian Radio (since its inception in 1995). I could not be bothered to change the station, thinking, "*As long as they are not 'talking rubbish' I will be fine.*"

I could not ignore the next snippet as the then Secretary of State for Education, Rt. Hon. Michael Gove was interviewed about new types of schools that would reshape the nation's education landscape. He talked about people who had been sponsored to visit other countries, including the United States, to study this concept. He made reference to a group of professionals undertaking an innovative programme called Future Leaders, whom he believed had the passion and training to make the proposed schools work. As I listened, something leapt in my heart.

This is an answer to my prayers. This is what God wants me to get involved with! I thought with excitement.

All I could do for the rest of the journey was dialogue with God about what I believed He was telling me. I had been part of the Future Leaders' training programme, a specialist selective course to develop headteachers for challenging inner-city schools, since 2008. Now, I was flooded with questions. "*How will this work? What happens next?*"

St. Mary's Church of England School, Hendon, was based on two sites within walking distance of each other. Downage housed departments like Science, English and Maths as well as Key stage 3 students; while the other, Sunnyfields housed Humanities, Key stages 4 and 5. As Deputy Headteacher on a Future Leader's headship residency, I had line management responsibilities for Year 9, Geography and Science, all based in Downage, but I taught Key Stages 4 and 5 Science in Sunnyfields. As a senior member of staff, I also had other duties on both sites. I spent my break duty speaking to God under my breath as I walked around the playground at Sunnyfields. My trips between Downage and Sunnyfields had a different emphasis that day. My focus and prayer became "*Lord, open the door. Show me what to do next.*"

A few days later, I got a phone call from the Future Leaders' office informing me that the CEO Heath Monk was organising a meeting with the Secretary of State for Education and some Future Leaders participants, to discuss Mr. Gove's ideas about schools. Since I had been going on about small school concepts, would I be available to attend the meeting? My response was, 'Certainly! Please let me have the dates with enough notice to get time off.' I was excited about the prospect of considering the ideas about small schools and other opportunities for improving education for young people in our inner-city schools. I kept this information to myself and decided to wait till I received the invitation to understand what was happening.

I got the invitation to the event at the Department for Education (DfE) to discuss next steps. The meeting was to take place at the Sanctuary Buildings on Great Smith Street in London. The event on July 20, 2010, from 11:30am to 1pm, was described as a "Meeting for supportive Future Leaders". The courtyard was flooded with light from the roof glass. As we were ushered upstairs, I was fascinated by the interior glass structure and plant arrangements that brought back lovely memories of the beauty I experienced at the Eden Project in Cornwall some years earlier. As the lift moved up, I focused on the building, trying to understand which features would qualify it as a listed building – the courtyard, location, structure, etc. I decided to name it *The Glass House*, my nickname for the Headquarters of the Department for Education.

Within a few minutes of arriving in the meeting room, the secretary of state for Education, Rt. Hon. Gove walked in with other dignitaries including The Rt Hon. Lord Adonis (then Member of Parliament and Schools Minister); and Lord Hill of Oareford – the incumbent Parliamentary Under-Secretary (Department for Education). Everyone in the room had something exciting to say and some seemed to have it all figured out.

Apart from introductions, I determined not to say anything more than necessary throughout. I was having an internal dialogue with God, letting Him know that He had not given me the next steps yet. It seemed the meeting was ending, and I thought it had been a good discussion about the future of education in Britain, until the Secretary of State turned to me.

"Titilayo, tell us about your dream school and what you think about the conversation so far."

This jolted me, then I felt instructed to open my mouth and let God fill it. So, I described the ideal small school based on Christian values. I talked about the journey of raising black boys in the East End of London, with all its struggles; the possibility of creating relevant, aspirational schools, where every child is nurtured to achieve their best, irrespective of their starting point. It seemed as if I was listening to someone else describe my dream school. Indeed, I had opened my mouth and it was being filled. I noticed that the entire room had their eyes fixed on me for however long it took to tell this story.

“What are you waiting for?” Mr Gove asked, when I finished. “What are the barriers stopping you from setting up these types of schools you have just described?”

I stammered for a few seconds. “Buildings, policies and legislation.”

“Unless it goes against the law of gravity, you have no excuses. And you have my full support to set up such schools.” Was his reply, or words to that effect.

It was the answer to my prayers about what to do next.

He went on to express how he wished he could capture the essence of that meeting in a bottle. Lord Adonis described the meeting as so inspiring that his last few sleepless nights over education issues were worthwhile.

I was excited as I pondered over the description of this school that emerged as I spoke. As soon as I got home, I said to my husband, "We are setting up a school."

His response was incredulous. "What school?"

I tried to replay the ideal school as I heard it in the meeting room.

Akin advised that I should pray a bit more and think of other options, possibly a private school, possibly in another country, but not here, not with the government. There was no precedent to this (sponsors of new schools previously had to have prior funding of £2 Million).

As though I did not hear what he was saying, I continued giving him more details about this school: the type of children it would cater for, the culture, on and on I went. Again, it was like listening to someone else talking to me about the school.

This was when the reality of establishing a new Christian school crystallized into a vision and a mission to be accomplished in my mind.

2

FUTURE LEADERS

Enrolment into Future Leaders was my route to headship. At least, that was what I thought when I started in January 2008. As the journey progressed, the approach of setting up a new school emerged, helped along by the challenges and constraints I experienced in securing a suitable employment position on completing my residency.

I initially did not set out to be a headteacher. I was more than content as Head of Learning in a very large secondary school. But there were several issues, so I prayed and kept thinking of ways to make things better, both for students and teachers. The more I prayed, the more restless I became. The excitement of being able to introduce new initiatives, work through them and see the positive impact on students, teachers, and parents became my driver for going into school daily – to make a difference to the school community.

As I prayed about the projects, the students, and the school, I found myself being more vocal about any and everything that could be done better. The thoughts of becoming a headteacher crossed my mind, and I rigorously tried to send those far from me, however, the rationale persisted that I could achieve more from a position of influence, not only with students and teachers, but with the school community. I eventually reached a deal with God (to be re-assured that these were not just my thoughts going wild, and that He would help me through this). If God would fulfil five criteria that I had researched and convinced myself were impossible, then I would entertain the thought of becoming a headteacher and be the best I possibly could. My list included such ideas as the following:

To be an excellent headteacher:

- *I want to be mentored and coached by practicing headteachers – possibly people with a Christian faith conviction.*
- *I want to learn how to lead a school through academic work, such as attending lectures to learn from others.*
- *I want the opportunity to 'practice' being a headteacher, just like doctors have residency.*

- *I want the principles and values of my faith to underpin my decisions, and to gain experience about best practice in education from other parts of the world.*
- *I want to go through a rigorous competitive selection process to start the journey.*

If God ticked these boxes, only then would I entertain this thought. Certain that my five requirements were all impossible to accomplish (*did I forget that nothing is impossible with God? Thinking back, it appears I just might have*), I decided to ignore the restlessness and make the best of my day-to-day work.

A few weeks after writing out the requirements, my pastoral deputy in school came across some information he felt I would be interested in. He was inclined to register my name but wanted to clarify it with me first. I did not pay attention to his request until he left some documentation on my desk with a note encouraging me to register an interest.

> Thank you for your interest in the Future Leaders programme.
>
> Future Leaders is a movement to develop senior leaders for challenging urban secondary schools. We are seeking exceptional current or former teachers with Qualified

Teacher Status, strong leadership potential, and above all, a passion to make a difference in some of the most challenging secondary schools in London. We believe that, with our training and support, you could be thriving as a senior leader in a challenging school in twelve months, and achieving headship within four years.

We offer:

- A year-long paid apprenticeship under an urban headteacher
- Cutting-edge training and personal development tailored to the urban school context
- Coaching and mentoring from a professional tutor and an ex-headteacher coach
- Bespoke career support and assistance in becoming a senior leader, then a Headteacher
- Guidance through NPQH
- The opportunity to see and share best practice in urban schools in the UK and USA.

We are currently recruiting within London and Greater Manchester. If you would like to find out more, do attend an information session, where you will get the chance to meet the recruitment team and some of our current participants, and have any questions answered. …"

Here is the response I got when I finally registered.

"I knew you could overturn all my objections," I said to the Lord. "But I was not expecting you to do so, so quickly. Well, there are still hurdles to cross. I am not even sure I will be accepted."

Not really convinced, I attended the evening information session held at Adam Street in London on Wednesday 13th February 2008 with Bernadette, my friend and colleague from the same school. There was a short overview and presentation, and time to talk to people who were on the programme.

After the event and a good conversation with Bernadette, who was convinced that God wanted me to apply for this programme, I decided to give it a try. She constantly reminded me of the Friday deadline for the online application, and I re-assured her I would submit it in time. Somehow, I did not even start, let alone complete the form. I felt really bad that I had given Bernadette my word but made no effort to start the application process. Then my husband caught the bug of nagging me about it, but my weekend was so busy that I did not get round to the form until Sunday night. The deadline was past, but I still felt the need to console myself that I had completed it. It was so late that my husband insisted on bringing the laptop into our bedroom for me to do so.

I completed every section, read over my notes, and pressed "submit" at about three minutes to midnight with a sigh of relief, certain it was not for me, since the deadline was Friday. The words that appeared on the screen left me astonished and amused at God's sense of humour. The deadline had been shifted to midnight! If the application was successful, Future Leaders would get in touch within two weeks and applicants would proceed to the next stage. I received a reply three days later.

After other assessment activities, including aptitude tests, case studies and essay writing, I was really pleased to receive an email on Monday 3rd March confirming that I was through to the next stage, an assessment on 20th March at The Resource Centre, 356 Holloway Road, London N7.

I was unable to make weekdays as my headteacher was adamant that I would not be granted permission. Eventually, my assessment took place on Saturday 5th April 2008 from 12:30 till 4:30pm. Future Leaders had arranged a special day for those of us who could not make the earlier dates. This included candidates who had travelled from France.

My invitation stated that I did not need to bring or prepare anything, but Bernadette, who went with me, insisted on giving me a mock interview. We talked about the issues of disadvantaged students, practical ways to ensure their progress, and how to lead a school with vision and values. We also discussed the impact of some work we had done, through the London Challenge programme, on the progress of our students.

When I was called in, I was re-assured that I had a friend sitting downstairs praying for me during this process. It was as though she had the interview questions beforehand, and our conversations were indeed my preparation! There were some answers I might not have given as candidly without that earlier conversation downstairs.

"*Dear God, you are at it again!*" was my thought. "*At this stage, I do not have any reason to doubt that you want me to embark on this journey. Please guide me all the way.*" I prayed.

On 26th May 2008, I was welcomed on the Future Leaders journey with this email:

> *"Congratulations on joining the 2008 cohort of Future Leaders! We are delighted to have you on board and are looking forward to working with you over the coming years in forging a network of strong urban leaders, all committed to improving the life chances of some of London's most disadvantaged pupils."*

I read the email repeatedly, with mixed feelings. I was excited but fearful of what I had led myself into. However, there was also the confidence that God would journey through this unknown future with me. I was embarking on a great adventure.

Dear

As you will be aware, (participant 2008) has been successful in his/ her application to Future Leaders, a leadership programme to develop senior leaders for challenging urban schools.

This intensive programme will commence this summer with 17 days of training delivered at the National College for School Leadership in Nottingham. Ten days of this training will be held during school holidays in August. However, in order to fully prepare our participants for their first year of residency as a senior leader, we have also planned one Saturday and a long weekend in June and one long weekend in July (20th - 22nd June and 11th - 13th July). Whilst we know that this is still term time, we would be very grateful if you would give permission for (participant 2008) to attend two essential days of training on Friday 20th June and Friday 11th July. If you need to discuss this matter, please make contact via our schools' network manager. (**Name and contact no. redacted**)

If you would like your school to be involved in Future Leaders, we would really like to hear from you. You might like to find out more about the programme online at www.future-leaders.org.uk.

Many thanks for your understanding and support.

Kind regards,

Heath Monk

As part of the third cohort of Future Leaders, I had to sign the contract to start a four-year training programme, relinquish my permanent job and take on a one-year training post, after which I could apply for senior leadership roles. I was hopeful that, despite the risks and uncertainties associated with this move, it would be worth it in the end. A letter was sent to our headteachers like the one below.

I thought this letter signed by Heath Monk, the CEO of Future Leaders, was more than enough for my headteacher to release me. After all, this was an opportunity to develop myself and add value to others. I was in for a shock when I was called into the head's office one nice bright morning (you are not normally called into the head's office for pleasant things, especially as a pastoral leader. Instead, when students in your year group have done something wrong, let the side down, or disgraced the school, you are called in to answer for them or to "sort things out"). Within seconds, I found out that I had committed the "unheard of act of seeking to do something so important without permission", according to the headteacher. This was echoed by the assistant headteacher, who was supposed to have guided and shown me the courses to apply for and the right pathway for my career progression.

It was made very clear that I was having ideas beyond my station. My experience that day was weird. The headteacher paced up and down, telling me how every effort would be made to stop me from my foolishness. Future Leaders would be informed about "all you have done wrong!" It was like watching an infuriated dragon about to swipe me into oblivion with its tail. The imagery was so real that I shut my eyes tight and crouched low to avoid the swipe of the dragon's tail. I had my back pressed very hard to the door as though hoping it would open to let me out. When I opened my eyes and slowly stood up, I was not sure what the two ladies thought, as they sent me out of the office with a declaration of failure. I guess that was supposed to convince me not to go ahead with the plans.

I was prepared to submit my resignation letter, but it had to go through the line manager to the head teacher. My line manager insisted that the resignation be accompanied with a "thank you" letter and flowers. I managed the "thank you" letter but could not bring myself to buy the flowers. The last half term was difficult as I struggled to understand what was going on around me. As part of the preparation for the Future Leaders programme, we needed to contact and visit schools to secure a school for our residency, a year of working with a head teacher as our mentor. My school would not permit me to carry out these visits. The ones I managed to organize were after school hours. Meanwhile, the headteacher tasked me, via my line manager, to hand write an A4 page (minimum) report for each child in my year group (about 360 of them) sitting facing the wall in my line manager's office.

I eventually got a residency school in North London on the last day of the academic year. The school was empty and the head teacher was rather relaxed, in trainers. Only then did I realize that the school was closed but the head chose to see me. The meeting was very different from some other meetings where I was told that, though the school had an influx of ethnic minority children, the senior members of staff were not prepared to work with people like me. I later found out that this school had a Future Leaders participant in residency; so, the concept was not new to the head teacher.

I was particularly happy as this gave me the opportunity to work in the Church school I had longed for. My residency was in a Church of England School!

3

THE BID FOR A NEW SCHOOL

I began to research and write out what an excellent school would look like. *What characteristics should it have? Above all, how would godly values shape the lives of students who attend the school?* The concept of having a school that is very much part of its local community made me think of the communities I was part of. I had previously lived and worked in the London Borough of Waltham Forest, where my church was located. The socio-economic and demographic characteristics of this part of East London matched the criteria of areas in need of new schools.

My preparation involved researching the characteristics of Walthamstow, London, to further understand the people, their needs and how we could "serve the community relevantly" through the establishment of a school. The more I wrote and researched, the clearer it became that I needed to involve other people, so I decided to share the vision with my pastor, Reverend Doug Williams. Doug is the senior pastor of the Emmanuel Christian Centre (ECC), a church that has existed in the local area for several decades and been involved in various activities, including running a day nursery for over 25 years as part of its mission to support people in need.

In 2005, the Church Trustees decided that an additional charitable trust was needed to oversee all community outreaches from the church. Therefore, they established The Greenleaf Trust (GT) as the outward facing entity to meet the needs of people in the London Borough of Waltham Forest and beyond. The church wanted to represent Christ in the locality through practical support such as providing homes for the homeless. As one of the founding directors of The Greenleaf Trust, I thought the various community activities and projects running under the Trust and by ECC formed a good foundation for the church to support the establishment of a school. The ECC community had expertise and experience in running children and youth work activities, both during term-time and holidays.

We held several meetings with the elders, then with trustees and several stakeholders in the church. There were mixed reactions as people contemplated the magnitude of the challenge. Some felt it was impossible, others advised us to keep church business to church, while some were encouraging and even offered to assist. Some of the responses and feelings could be summarized in the words of this email:

> *"Is it possible to somehow put in a nutshell what exactly we as a board of trustees/directors/whatever, are getting ourselves into? Please forgive me if this sounds like paranoia, but in the overall enthusiasm, can we make sure that the free school does not gradually overwhelm either the overall wider vision of ECC/GT or surreptitiously take over the life of any one of us?"*

Alongside meetings within the church, I attended meetings with local community groups and politicians to get their opinion and where possible, seek support for the project. It is worth noting that, in 2010, the UK's government, led by Prime Minister David Cameron (through a coalition between Conservatives and Liberal Democrats) halted the Labour government's flagship school building programme. The latter had embarked on a very ambitious investment called 'Building Schools for the Future' (BSF), a capital project worth about £55 Billion, which was aimed at providing or improving educational facilities, such that every child would be taught in a state-of-the-art building. In 2010, London Borough of Waltham Forest had its portion of the 'Building Schools for the Future' blocked by the new coalition government, prompting protests and a subsequent legal challenge. This created a contentious political environment and strained relationships between local government and the Department for Education (DfE), not to mention the political differences between the two.

Preparation for our first bid involved meetings with DfE officials (Katie Halliday, James Valance, William Thursfield) in their HQ in Westminster (the Glass House), site visits to our proposed shortlist of properties in the E17 postcode area, as well as helpful input from New Schools Network (Helen Cameron and Rachel Wolf). New Schools Network, (NSN) was founded by Rachel Wolf, a former adviser to Boris Johnson and Michael Gove. She started the group after visiting New York City and observing the city's charter schools as well as groups such as the Knowledge Is Power Program (KiPP) and the New York City Charter School Center, who advise new schools in the city.

We eventually submitted a bid in the spring of 2010 as part of the first wave of free school applications. We then waited in vain for a response (promised in a few weeks). On further enquiry, we were told that the appropriate person to deal with the application was on holiday, so the bid was not processed in time for the deadline. What a setback!

In the autumn of 2010, Education Secretary Michael Gove announced that 16 proposals for free schools had been given a green light by the Government and were expected to open in September 2011. Five of these 16 were faith schools – one Evangelical Anglican, one Hindu, one Sikh and two Jewish schools. Eventually, only 24 out of 306 proposals were approved to open in 2011 – this first set were also known as Wave 1 of the Free Schools programme in the UK.

Subsequently, we received news that the process for the next tranche was being overhauled and we would have to wait for new guidelines. These were not published until March 2011 and stipulated a submission date of end of May 2011. Proposers would have to set up a compliant charitable company to run the new schools, implying that we could no longer use The Greenleaf Trust as in the previous bid. The new guidelines stated that the new Trust would specifically provide education, not a mix of community activities.

I wrote to the church trustees as follows:

"Dear all,

We received the long- awaited application details from the Department for Education. Some of the details are indicated below from the New Schools Network. Please note the deadline and the requirement for the business case to be completed as part of the submission. Some salient points to note include the following:

- *A new Academy Trust will be required specifically for the school*
- *We need a governing body with an active designated chair of governors*
- *For a Faith school we need a letter of endorsement from the relevant religious body (AOG National) – perusal of the new requirements indicate that it will be more advantageous for us to apply for a Faith school.*

The new form requires more details and rigour, so we need TEAMS of experts to work on various aspects of the form."

I also called for a workshop on Saturday 2nd April 2011 at the Greenleaf Building.

The race to set up the new company in time became a story on its own. A childhood friend, Mrs. Debo Sokoya, who works as a chartered secretary, offered to co-ordinate the memorandum and articles of association in compliance with DfE's model templates for Academy trusts. Even when we used Companies House's accelerated route for setting up the company swiftly, there were a few tense days following news that Companies House had not received the submitted documents. Ultimately, crossed wires were untangled and *The Emmanuel School Trust* (TEST) was duly registered on 19th May 2011 with three founding directors: Rev. Anthony Hodgkinson, Mr. Ernest Osafo and Dr Akin Oluwatudimu. We were very relieved and grateful to God. This was a watershed moment in the journey, as it marked the birth of a new faith designate trust to run Christian faith schools in the UK.

Preparing the Free school bid was a major undertaking. I felt constrained to relinquish full-time work, so I worked freelance as an educational consultant for this period to deliver the required outcomes. My husband and I, as well as members of the task group, attended various workshops and training events set up for free school proposers. We collated survey information, research data and administered questionnaires to assess the interest of local families in sending children to our new school. As Lead Proposer of the bid for what we christened 'Emmanuel Community School', I was the main contact for the DfE, liaising between the department and the volunteers that made up our bid team.

The application bid was prepared in strict compliance with the guidance from DfE and NSN. The bid document eventually consisted of 141 pages in A4 format, typed double-spaced, and with appendices.

The Members and Directors confirmed to the DfE in the bid (submitted in May 2011) included the following: proposed Chair of the Governing Body, REV. ANTHONY HODGKINSON (company Member and director); MR. ERNEST OSAFO, (company Member and director), DR. AKIN OLUWATUDIMU (company Member and director); REV. DOUGLAS C. WILLIAMS, MR. PETER LEWIS, MRS. HILDA JACKSON, MRS. LAURAINE COLTHART, and MRS. TITILAYO OLUWATUDIMU, Lead Proposer and Principal Designate.

Members and Directors

Please confirm the total number of (a) Company Directors [3] and (b) any other members of the Governing Body [5] appointed to date and list them below. Please also confirm who the proposed Chair of the Governing Body is.

Name: REVD. ANTHONY HODGKINSON

Position: DIRECTOR

Name: MR. ERNEST OSAFO

Position: DIRECTOR

Name: DR. AKIN OLUWATUDIMU

Position: DIRECTOR

Name: REVD. DOUGLAS C. WILLIAMS

Position: MEMBER

Name: MR. PETER LEWIS

Position: MEMBER

Name: MRS. HILDA JACKSON

Position: MEMBER

Name: MRS. LAURAINE COLTHART

Position: MEMBER

Name: MRS. TITILAYO OLUWATUDIMU

Position: MEMBER & PRINCIPAL DESIGNATE

In addition to pulling the revised bid together, it was necessary to address the constraints associated with the 'faith school' designation and the government's stipulation that faith concepts should not be taught as a 'science'. Religious beliefs were to be confined to appropriate sections of the curriculum, rather than being imposed on children as facts. There were guidance documents and FAQs from DfE, directing proposers away from using schools as a platform for indoctrination or proselytising their faith values. Applicants who wished to establish faith schools had the option of a 'faith ethos' or a 'faith designation'. We discussed our required stance with our

DfE lead contact, as well as with the New Schools Network, among others.

This matter formed one of the controversial issues which Rev. George Hargreaves, a minister and member of the Christian Alliance party, raised with the Rt. Hon. Michael Gove at one of the early conferences to promote the government's free schools' agenda.

Extract from New Schools Network Guidance for Free school applicants

Faith ethos

Faith ethos is explained in the glossary of the DfE's How to Apply Guidance. Adopting a faith ethos is a way of explicitly aligning your school with a particular faith. The principles of that faith can shape your vision for the school and its ethos. However, a school with a faith ethos cannot:

- Provide religious education and collective worship in line with your chosen faith, if this is anything other than Christian in nature (unless the school has successfully applied to the Secretary of State for an exemption);
- Adopt faith-based admission arrangements; or

- Recruit teachers on the basis of faith unless it can be justified as a genuine occupational requirement (e.g., in the case of the principal designate or RE teacher).

Faith designation

Faith designation is explained in the glossary of the DfE's How to Apply Guidance. Obtaining a faith designation means that your school can more overtly uphold the tenets of your chosen religion. Faith designation is a legal recognition that your school has a religious character. You only need to do this if you intend to:

- Provide religious education and collective worship according to the tenets of the faith of the school; and/or
- Give preference when appointing teachers to those of the same faith as the school; and/or
- Admit up to 50% of pupils on the basis of faith if your school is oversubscribed.

Having a faith designation will mean that you involve the appropriate religious authority which will inspect the provision of religious education and advise on admissions. You could also involve them at a governance level.

Ref.

https://www.newschoolsnetwork.org/sites/default/files/Faith%20Free%20Schools%20January%202019_0.pdf

#

The bid was supported with detailed research findings on the demography, educational attainment, and socio-economic characteristics of the area to be served by the school. It also clarified the educational plan, curriculum, leadership and staffing structure, budget projections and governance.

In writing the bid, I received much invaluable assistance from a range of sources, including numerous seminars, workshops, and conferences by DfE, legal firms and a range of others, all aimed at equipping and informing free school and academy proposers. There was also the earlier cited New Schools Network. In addition, we benefitted from pro-bono support from a range of firms and organisations. My husband and I collated all the required information and typed the proposal bid, with many iterations as each section took shape. Effectively, free schools called for a different approach from other state funded schools and were required to address and rectify the failures and inadequacies of the education system. Innovative thinking was called for, rather than business as usual.

Mr. Andy and Mrs. Lauraine Colthart of J'Harts Graphic Design, a local printing business and committed members of Emmanuel Christian Centre devoted substantial effort and time to the typesetting, printing, collating, and binding of the paper copies. Hilda Jackson, a teacher also dedicated time and effort to promoting the school bid and contributed many ideas. We gathered to pray over the copies, following which they were dispatched by registered post to the DfE. Electronic copies were also e-mailed to the DfE's designated mailbox before the deadline.

As much as the directors and members would have liked to take a break after submission in May, it was necessary to continue the public enlightenment and awareness campaign and build up the evidence of demand. The DfE wanted us to produce signed documents showing people's commitment to sending their children to the school when it opened; although we had to let them know that the school might not open if we did not get the Funding Agreement signed by the Secretary of State for Education. One of the conditions for getting the Secretary of State to sign a Funding Agreement was to provide evidence that a 'sufficient' number of children were signed up to attend the school, to make it viable, which depended on the total number of students expected to enrol.

Interviews of short-listed bidders were scheduled to take place in August, and we were really thrilled and thankful to God to receive an invitation to attend. The implication was that out of applications submitted for 2012 opening, 217 were rejected and ours was one of only 55 to progress to interview stage. As part of the process, I had to attend an assessment centre. Our interview was booked for Friday 12th August 2011. Lauraine had already notified us that she would be out of the country around this time and DfE wanted six people at the interview, including the Chair of the Trust (a role Akin offered to fill). As part of the preparation, we had our line up as follows:

1. Ernest – Finance/business
2. Titilayo – overall vision & principal designate
3. Peter – curriculum & operational issues
4. Hilda – ditto + local knowledge
5. Anthony or Doug – governance
6. Akin – governance, project management & facilities

Hurried preparations were made for the interview, including a detailed trial run/mock interview arranged with one of our advisers. We were all exhorted to master the bid documentation – all 141 pages of it.

While preparing for the interview, I received the email below from Future Leaders:

> *Dear Titilayo Oluwatudimu*
>
> ***FLCT Free Schools Principal Designate Assessment Centre***
>
> *As Principal Designate for a proposed Free School, you have been invited to attend an assessment and development centre being run by Future Leaders Charitable Trust (FLCT) on behalf of the Department for Education (DfE). I am writing to give you further information about the assessment.*
>
> *Future Leaders Charitable Trust is an organisation best known for its accelerated school leadership programme of the same name (www.future-leaders.org.uk) and through running this programme since 2006, we have developed expertise in recruiting and training future headteachers and principals. Our assessment activities are renowned for their rigorous and challenging nature, designed to identify the best potential leaders. We assess against a comprehensive competency framework which*

has been created following research into the qualities of effective leaders (an overview is attached for your information, and we recommend you familiarise yourself with this document before taking part in the assessment). We have been commissioned by the DfE to assess the leadership potential of Principal Designates for proposed Free Schools.

Working closely with the DfE we will deliver a thorough assessment centre. The assessment activities will give you the chance to stretch yourself and show yourself at your best. FLCT will make recommendations to the DfE following your assessment, and you will receive your results from the DfE by the end of September 2011. At this time, you will receive an assessment report and have the option to take part in a feedback session which will give you the opportunity to reflect on and discuss your strengths and development areas.

Details of the assessment activities are below. Please note that by proceeding, you consent to the content of your assessment activities and your results being shared with both the DfE and your free school trustee(s)/ sponsor(s).

The assessment centre will last for half a day and will consist of the following activities:

- *Behavioural Event Interview*
  This will be a 'one on one' interview with one of our assessors and will last for approximately two hours.

- *Presentation*
  This will be an individual activity. You will be given a topic on the day, and you will be required to prepare and deliver a presentation on this topic to the assessment panel.

- *Cognitive tests*
  You will complete three computer-based tests which look for a minimum level of cognitive ability. You will have the opportunity to complete some practice questions for each test online before the main testing session. Please ensure you have reading glasses with you if you need them.

On the day of the interview in August 2011, a group of us met at Wanstead Church Primary School in East London, where Peter was headteacher. It was a convenient meeting point and a short walking distance to Wanstead underground station where we boarded the tube and headed for Westminster. As we marched towards the 'Glass House' from Westminster tube station, Big Ben greeted us with the 9am chime that sounded like, "Welcome to this phase of God's plan!" Anthony joked that Big Ben had just indicated that the next three hours could shape history (little did we realize how true that would turn out to be).

We stopped at the coffee shop in Methodist Central Hall, Westminster, where we were joined by Akin Oluwatudimu, who had travelled a different route. While we waited to be served, some people walked in, and a smartly dressed young man among them greeted me cheerfully, excitedly introducing me to the others as his science teacher at Globe Academy. I was at Globe Academy as an Assistant Principal, Head of School of Maths and Science for a short period. Although I was his teacher for barely half a year, the young man eagerly told me about his undergraduate course, expressed his appreciation for my encouraging him, and introduced himself to other members of our team. I took this as encouragement from the Lord that, acts of diligence, no matter how short the duration, can be worthwhile, and also, that God was smiling over this project. In other words, even when faced with a daunting task or lack of adequate resources, great outcomes are possible.

At the Glass House, we were escorted upstairs to the meeting room, where we noticed that the upholstery in the room was the colour we had selected for our school (the school uniform sample Hilda had brought with her matched perfectly!). She commented that this could be a good sign that the DfE appreciated our school colour, which made us feel more at ease. After some introductions and pleasantries, the interview began in earnest and went on for about ninety minutes. Although our names were boldly written on cards in front of each of us, the DfE officials kept referring to Ernest Osafo (the finance director) as my spouse, and we had to correct them several times. (It was only later, when we got the feedback that we realised they had wrongly assumed we were proposing a setup in which I would be Principal Designate, with my husband Akin as Finance Director!)

We left the place with a sense of victory, knowing that the Lord had helped us so far, and the rest was in His hands. We were excited that the days of preparation and mock interview had paid off. Most of the questions and scenarios raised during the interview were what we had prepared for. We went back to the Westminster coffee shop to pray before dispersing in different directions.

After the excitement and adrenalin rush of the run-up to the interview in August and the subsequent Future Leaders Assessment, Monday 10th October 2011 proved a very confusing day for me as I received the feedback report from the free school assessment centre with the instruction to forward the letter and report to the Academy Trust. It read as follows:

"10 October 2011

Dear Emmanuel Community School Academy Trust,

I understand that you will by now have received written confirmation of the Department for Education's decision about your application to establish a Free School. As part of the application process, your preferred candidate for appointment to the post of Principal Designate took part in a Future Leaders Charitable Trust (FLCT) assessment centre. On the basis of their performance against the range of competencies set out in the attached report, we do not consider your candidate suitable for appointment at this time. This recommendation has been shared with the Department however, it was not a determining factor in the Department's final decision on your Free School application. Beyond providing an independent recommendation on your candidate's suitability for appointment, FLCT had no role to play in the Free School application process. There is no recourse for making an appeal against the assessment centre findings however if you wish to discuss the qualitative assessment in the attached, please contact us to arrange a convenient time for a discussion.

Yours sincerely Future Leaders Charitable Trust

"As discussed at interview it is important that a husband and wife as members of the Trust (as in your school's case) avoid any potential conflicts of interest and in particular do not have sole control over the school's finances if they work together as accounting officer and finance director respectively. As we discussed, the current arrangement set out in your application is not good governance practice, will potentially give rise to conflicts of interest and does not allow for appropriate separation of duties. The approval of your application is therefore conditional on you confirming with us your actions on this issue and you will need to provide amended governance arrangements that meet with our approval.

"We recommend that you run an open recruitment process for this post to ensure you get the right candidate for this key appointment."

Despite the underwhelming note from Future Leaders, our spirits soared when, on October 12, 2011, the DfE gave the green light for Emmanuel Community School to proceed to the next stage of the free school process which is the pre-opening stage – WE WERE THROUGH!

We received a congratulatory letter from the Secretary of State for Education. The approval, however, came with three DfE conditions, one of which was an anti-climax and a potential showstopper. Based on the report submitted by the Future Leaders' assessor, I was not to apply to lead the school as the principal designate. By definition, the Principal Designate is the appointed head of the school who will guide its development through the pre-opening phase, and then run the school as head once it opens. I had been the 'Lead Proposer' of the school bid proposal and was really pleased that we had come this far. Nevertheless, the DfE required a formal response from our Trust to the three conditions they imposed by 24th October 2011 (within two weeks) if the bid were to progress further.

The DfE approval to proceed to the pre-opening phase was followed by several meetings within the team and with our key stakeholders. One of the key challenges was the very tight timescale. The government had set a target of 12 months for the new school to be opened (i.e., September 2012) against the backdrop of political and logistical hurdles that we needed to overcome, not least of which was to secure appropriate premises and recruit staff and students. We became acutely aware of the uncertainty of opening the school during this period, making it difficult to make certain decisions, including the appointment of a head teacher. In the pursuit of an appropriate response to this dilemma, I sought legal advice on the 20th of October. I was clear that I did not want to jeopardise the project, but how would we progress with these conditions, and what response should we prepare for the next DfE meeting on October 24th?

4

THE PRE-OPENING PHASE

As part of our collaborative work with the community, the team met with several councillors and local authority officials. However, we had difficulty securing an appointment with our local MP. After several attempts, members of our team finally met with Ms. Stella Creasy MP on 18th of November 2011. A colleague described the meeting as "rather interesting in a weird manner, with some food for thought". Our MP seemed to imply that our plan was to put children in pet shops and offices. She was not keen on our school proposal and went on to question the extent to which we even understood what it meant to be a qualified teacher! On reflection, this probably indicated the Labour party's stance, which she represented. The party opposed the Free School initiative of the Conservative/Liberal Democrat coalition government. Trade unions and other opponents were also largely critical of the scheme, highlighting the perceived shortcomings of the education policy championed by then Prime Minister Rt. Hon. David Cameron MP, and his Secretary of State Rt. Hon. Michael Gove MP.

At each significant step in the journey, our church congregation was informed of the bid's progress and the various issues to be resolved, and prayer support was sought. We also sought collaboration and support from other local churches and community groups. At the end of one prayer meeting in January 2012, Rev. Chris Palmer, the children's pastor at ECC, shared his impression of the next few months for me.

Paraphrasing, "*the next nine months will be like a pregnant woman with all the associated experiences. Sometimes frustration, etc. God has given you all that you need to cope. It is not about you, not for you but for Him and for His glory. Get a group of people to pray for you regularly*".

The advert to recruit our first head teacher (Principal Designate) went live on the school website and the Times Educational Supplement (TES) on November 11, 2011. Immediately the advert was posted, I was required to reassure DfE that I was not applying for the post. There were several phone calls back and forth, right down to the wire to ensure that I did not and was not intending to apply! Meanwhile, I had to make sure that the recruitment and selection process was administered properly, advertised nationally, with every stage of the process overseen by a DFE representative. Ian Gurman, an experienced educator and member of ECC came on board to facilitate the recruitment exercise. We had four applicants for the post. The shortlisting process involved fact-checking every section of each candidate's form with the DFE representative at the Greenleaf Centre. The exercise lasted several hours, after which candidates were chosen for the interview stage.

Interviews for the head teacher position took place on February 6th 2012 and involved a number of people from various aspects of Education and the community. Our Education Adviser from DfE, Sue Phillips was present as an observer. The day started with her clarifying again that I would not be applying for the post, and I wondered why she expected me to want to apply after witnessing the process so far. Moreover, I had clarified my decision in writing after she called a few days earlier with the same request. DfE also noted the risks associated with this appointment and the contingencies to be implemented if the proposed school did not open after all.

A week later, we announced the appointment of Mr. Peter Lewis as the first head teacher at Emmanuel Community School (ECS) Walthamstow. With a head teacher finally in place, we opened the admission process for students, months after the deadline, but still with no idea where the school would be located. The principal designate appointment was a celebratory landmark which was published on our new temporary website – theproposedemmanuelcommunityschool.co.uk – created to provide general information about the proposed school and updates for stakeholders and the public. This website address is defunct as a permanent one was subsequently set up when the school opened in 2012.

The government's free school and academies programme required new schools to be up and running within a short time frame. Academy trusts were given a development grant and required to avail themselves of expert consultants to cover the whole range of competencies, to ensure the new school would deliver its lofty objectives. While preparing our bid, we had received pro-bono support from various experts, however the pre-opening phase required formal appointments and contracts. Tenders were put out and fee quotations sought for project management, education and legal advisers, marketing and communications, ICT support and construction experts, among others. Key among the companies we appointed were Place Group (Project manager), Stone King

(Solicitors), Appleyards (Education adviser) and CODA (Marketing experts).

The next few months flew past in a flurry of activities targeting both teachers and students. Recruitment for reception and year 1 teachers began in March 2012 through adverts with eTeach, an education recruitment website. Activities to attract prospective students included a stall in Walthamstow's shopping mall, Selborne Walk, beneath the Food Hall staircase. Saturday May 5th was spent playing the grainy amateur video my son produced, while handing out balloons to attract children, so we could talk to their parents about the new faith school opening in Walthamstow. Church members distributed flyers and talked to parents; the youth group (Youth Wave) staged music and dance sessions in the mall and open market square, at various times of the day. This attracted large audiences, presented a point of entertainment for shoppers and an opportunity to hand out flyers and publicize the proposed school. We repeated the activities on the 18th of May from 9:30 am till 3pm, with several enquiries from the public; some were keen to support while others wanted more information.

14th May saw the first Open Day for parents from 2 to 6pm at our church premises, Emmanuel Christian Centre, 102-106 Erskine Road, E17 6SA. Parents wanted to know where the school would be located, but we did not have a site. It was not until 25th May 2012 that we finally announced the current St Mary's C of E Primary School, The Drive, Walthamstow, E17 3BN, as the permanent location from 2013. This auspicious news was featured in the Waltham Forest Guardian.

We could tell parents where we would be in 2013, but not in September 2012. The search for temporary accommodation was ongoing. Our first newsletter was published on 15th of June and the first set of parents, carers and children for September's reception class met on 4th July at Erskine Road. The children went home with our brand-new book bags.

Lizzie Crow, a radio presenter, interviewed Pastor Doug Williams and me on Premier Christian Radio's Inspirational Breakfast Drive on Wednesday 4th July. We shared the story of our journey towards opening our new school in September. We articulated the aims, objectives and progress to date, asking the Christian community to pray for and support the school.

July continued with a recruitment drive to counter a real threat to the possibility of the school opening. It seemed every child in the area already had a school to attend, and the plan to open with a reception class and a year one class was looking more unattainable by the day. We visited nurseries, parks, day care centres, libraries, everywhere and anywhere we could, to engage with parents of children of the relevant school age.

In parallel with recruiting staff and students, there was the drive to secure suitable premises. There were encouraging words from the incumbent Leader of the Council, the late Councillor Chris Robbins, whom I had known when he was a governor at a local school where I had also been a staff governor. He took an active interest in our project and gave useful indications on what type of premises to look for, and who within the Borough would be in a position to assist. The Council had put up a number of its properties for sale in this period. Nevertheless, the search for premises took a while.

In the USA, the Charter Schools movement took an open-minded and unconventional approach to school buildings, making it possible to create successful schools in premises which would have hitherto been considered unacceptable. Drawing from their remarkable achievements, the UK government moved to remove town planning restrictions where possible, to allow schools to be established wherever there was a need. Of course, this attracted criticism from opponents who gave the government a hard time about 'wasting' public funds on new schools, while starving existing schools of funds to address dilapidated school buildings up and down the country. In view of the tight timescale for new schools to open in line with government guidance, many were eventually sited in temporary premises while searching for/erecting better suited or appropriate buildings and facilities.

It is worth noting that at the time our school bid was written in 2011, we became aware of a public consultation to expand St Mary's Church of England Primary School, Walthamstow, to a three-form entry school and relocate it to larger premises within the borough of Waltham Forest. We therefore proposed that the existing St Mary's school site should become our new school location. This was what we submitted to the DfE in our application, and were finally able to announce in May, following protracted negotiations between the Church of England Diocese, DfE and key stakeholders.

Ultimately, Emmanuel Community School – the name chosen by the team – was incubated in the Emmanuel Christian Centre. After many consultation meetings with our church community, we decided to "nurse" the school within the Church building during its first year. The new school would open with a single reception class, sharing the Erskine Road Building and its limited external play space with the ECC Nursery, which had operated from that building for many decades.

Our church leadership deserves much credit for agreeing to the proposal. It was a good thing that the church also owned another building – the Greenleaf centre on Greenleaf Road, Walthamstow, just around the corner from Erskine Road. A general meeting of the congregation was held to seek approval to the re-configuration of the church's spaces and activities for a fixed term of 12-24 months. Once approval was secured, the necessary legal agreements were drawn up by DfE lawyers for temporary use of the premises on terms agreed with the Church Council.

Of course, there were negotiations and adjustments all around to make this project successful. One of the mandatory steps in the journey to opening a school building is a pre-opening inspection undertaken by the government Office for Standards in Education, Children's Services and Skills (Ofsted). The four-hour Ofsted inspection of our temporary premises at ECC, Erskine Road, Walthamstow took place on Tuesday 10th July 2012. The inspector scrutinized our website, every policy, document, and the physical environment, including proposed refurbishment plans for the building. We had to wait for an official report but felt we had done everything needed at that stage of the plans.

Later that day, Lauraine and I attended an afternoon tea event organised by New Schools Network at the House of

Lords to celebrate and promote the government's free school and academies programme. It was attended by Michael Gove, MP and Lord Dolar Popat of Harrow, a member of the British House of Lords. We had to leave promptly to continue preparing for the Readiness to Open Meeting (ROM) on Friday 13th. This was another very important milestone: another interview at the 'Glass House', chaired by a senior DfE official, Mela Watts. Our headteacher gave a 10-minute presentation about the school, followed by questions about our readiness to open. Despite some tense moments and rather condescending words from DFE representatives, we left the meeting relieved that the project was given the green light.

We continued to recruit students, but also started hiring other teaching and non-teaching/support staff. On the 23rd of July, interviews were held to appoint our first Nursery Officer, Mrs. Gurman.

During the same month, building work started on our temporary site – Emmanuel Christian Centre on Erskine Road. With a September 2012 opening date as the target, it was necessary to modify the ECC building: to convert the main hall to temporary classrooms, create additional toilet facilities to suit the number of young children expected; as well as to improve the fire safety precautions and emergency ingress and escape provisions. This meant that the church offices, including the pastors, would move to the Greenleaf building, while the necessary adjustments were made. The tender for the work was won by City Square Solutions of Fenchurch Avenue, London. They were devoted to the task, completing the work on schedule. In addition, the Company Director took a personal interest in supporting the Trust and ECC's charitable activities.

August was a nail-biting month. Faced with the risk that the Funding Agreement (FA) might not be signed because we did not have the required number of students, we reviewed a range of scenarios. We called for prayer support from our community and continuously sought divine assistance on our knees in prayer.

As the count-down to September continued, an email from Jonathan Daniels of the DfE arrived requesting an urgent meeting. My initial reaction was to attend the meeting with a couple of people, but after phone calls to our project managers and DfE officials, I realised that we were in a critical situation. *Project Emmanuel* was now red! What else could we do?

We had CODA (our marketing company) walking the streets of Walthamstow, visiting each Children's centre and attending outdoor events to sign parents up. Everything remained 'subject to funding agreement'; how could parents send their kids to a school with no site or guaranteed opening?

I contacted the core members of the *Project Emmanuel* team (those who had worked on the bid and those who attended the DfE interview) and pleaded that as many as possible attend this meeting with Jonathan Daniels. In the meantime, to manage the risks associated with not achieving our target number of students, we went back to the drawing board to see what could be done with one class (30 students) instead of two, and the minimum number of children required to turn *Project Emmanuel* green. Led by Ernest Osafo, a chartered accountant and the trust Finance lead, the financial team spent several hours testing different scenarios. They eventually established the minimum number of pupils at which the new school could run within the projected grant income per student.

Tom Legge, a key member of the professional team from Place Group, suggested we provide DfE with a communication grid, a planning tool clarifying how communication issues for the subsequent pre-opening activities would be managed. I emailed this out to a few members for prayer support and comments. On the morning of the meeting with DfE, I was about to leave the house when I felt the need to print 10 copies of the communication grid. Not certain how this would fit into the agenda or how it could turn things around, I dropped my bag at the door, printed ten copies and stuffed them into my bag.

The meeting with Jonathan Daniels and other DfE officials took place in the Glass House, where he proceeded to lay down the hard facts. With the time at our disposal, the prospects of reaching the target student number of sixty was receding by the day, and it was now necessary to move to Plan B, if there was one. They asked if we had considered dropping from a two-form to a single-form entry school. Much as we were reluctant to do this, the scenario planning workshop our finance team had undertaken saved the day. We agreed with DfE to keep to one reception class of 30 students; but we were still far from that number. Our calculations indicated that *Project Emmanuel* would not be viable if the number of children enrolled in the first cohort fell below twenty. In addition, the funding agreement would not be signed if we did not have a minimum of twenty students to start the school.

The application forms came in, slowly enough for us to celebrate each one. The first one was from a girl named FAITH; we took this to be an encouragement. We needed faith to obtain the remaining nineteen application forms, and the 20th arrived at the last minute. We could not sign the DfE funding agreement documents until we received this form, which Hilda brought in about 8pm. The five copies were duly signed amidst great relief and joy. We celebrated as Andy Colthart gladly took photos, and Pastor Doug Williams insisted on wearing a suit and tie as he signed on behalf of TEST. The signed documents could now be presented for the Secretary of State's signature.

On Monday morning, I made my way to the Glass House, holding the signed documents close to my chest. I arrived around half-past ten, and the wait was interminable. A young man eventually came to collect the documents on behalf of Dominic Flitcroft, *Project Emmanuel*'s main contact within the DfE. I made him sign the delivery note, explaining that I was the courier service for the day, and I needed proof of delivery. He was rather amused by this.

Days later, I got a phone call – "TITILAYO, YOU ARE THROUGH! THE FUNDING AGREEMENT HAS BEEN SIGNED!"

On Thursday 9th August 2012, Dominic emailed saying a letter from Michael Gove MP confirming the Funding Agreement decision was in the post.

With great excitement I sent out this text message to friends and well-wishers.

"God's faithfulness is confirmed once again. The Secretary of State has signed the Funding Agreement for The Emmanuel School's Trust to run Emmanuel Community School for the next seven years (renewable). SPREAD THE GOOD NEWS!"

We later received the letter, which we framed with a photograph from the opening ceremony. It is on display as one of the artefacts of Emmanuel Community School's history.

Press coverage: - WALTHAMSTOW: New free school to open at St Mary's site - Sunday 27th May 2012. The school will open in temporary accommodation for one year at Emmanuel Christian Centre, 102-106 Erskine Road, E17 6SA.

5

THE NEW SCHOOL OPENS

On Monday 10th September 2012, Emmanuel Community School (ECS) opened its doors to our first reception class. We were operating from our temporary premises within Emmanuel Christian Centre.

The new students started lessons at 9am, following a week of staff In-Service Training (INSET). The school offered a warm welcome to the next generation of innovators, leaders, captains of industry, politicians, preachers, etc., in the main hall situated on the 1st floor of the building. The official opening took place the following week, on Wednesday 19th of September. For me, it was sobering to realise that dreams do come true. The seemingly far-fetched thought of setting up a Christian school in the heart of Walthamstow was now a reality! It was the beginning of great things to come, not the end of the journey. I was reassured that life still had a lot of wonders in store because "EVERYONE HAS A

FUTURE." This statement was adopted as the school motto.

It's worth backtracking a bit to clarify how we got that strapline. Since our church had a vibrant children's and youth ministry, we decided to run a competition among the children to come up with a motto for the new school. This winning entry, *Everyone Has a Future*, was by Adam Brown. The judges were impressed by how the statement portrayed the Trust's aim to ensure that each ECS student reached their full potential, irrespective of their background, ability or provenience.

At the opening ceremony in the Greenleaf Building, we sang "*This little light of mine*" – our very first performance by the reception cohort. We cut a cake decorated with our school's name and logo, had cupcakes with our school logo, and lots of finger foods. In attendance were many adults who had been part of setting up the school. The school logo, designed by J'Harts depicts a group of people joined together with raised hands around a book. Among other things, it depicts how knowledge brings joy and enthusiasm.

Although space would not permit the inclusion of a comprehensive list here, this rollcall of enablers includes the following categories:

- The ECC church leaders – principally Senior Pastor Douglas Williams, who became a trustee and school governor, and the Senior Assistant Pastor Anthony Hodgkinson, who was a founding member of the trust, as well as a trustee and school governor – despite a full diary of church activities and duties.
- The team of elders of the church and the trustees – who embraced the vision and facilitated the school's incubation in the church building.
- ECC – the church community – many of whom rolled up their sleeves as motivated volunteers to support the work.
- Our children's parents, guardians, and families – who put their faith in the trust and risked sending their children to attend a school that had just started.
- The local councillors of London Borough of Waltham Forest, who took an interest in the work of the church and its outreach activities. Of particular note was the support from Councillor Saima Mahmud and the late Chris Robbins, council leader.

- A wide range of formally appointed external consultants, and those who offered pro-bono contributions. These include Tom Legge, David Jenkins, Claire Delaney, and others from Place Group, Graham Burns from Stone King, and Clive Ledger from Appleyards, among others.
- Various officers from the DfE and New Schools Network.
- ECC's Children's pastor and youth leaders, along with the young people, many of whom were immensely passionate about making a positive impact on the community.

In October 2012, we held our first set of Open Days for 2013 admissions. Parents seeking admission for their pre-school children were invited to visit the school. We also had our first harvest festival, and the children were very good as they sang the harvest songs. The donations from the harvest event were sent to the Forest Churches Emergency Night Shelter initiative (FCENS), a local homeless project.

In November, our first class group photograph was published in the Waltham Forest Guardian and the term ended with the Christmas concert.

The team of adults who helped us through the first year include our Head Teacher (Mr. Lewis), our class teacher (Mrs. Jackson), Nursery Officer (Mrs. Gurman), Ms. Joseph, the office manager and volunteers, including Mrs. Lewis, Ms. Simpson, Mrs. Jackson, Ms. Fava, Mrs. Spencer and Mrs. Colthart as well as Mrs. Lee and Mrs. Nawaz, our mid-day supervisors. Ms. Morris was our music teacher, and Nick and Alison – breakfast and afterschool club staff.

The inaugural year went by quickly as we set up all the requisite policies, procedures, and operational details. Also, sharing the premises with ECC nursery called for logistical arrangements regarding access and egress, shared use of the playground and managing parental expectations. Mrs Jackson (Hilda) took a bold step in accepting the role of reception teacher and getting to grips with the Early Years Foundation Stage (EYFS) requirements, even though her experience was mainly of older children (key stage 2). Dorothy Spence, an experienced school leader, joined the team and worked closely with our headteacher Peter Lewis. We also felt the need to engage an experienced School Improvement Partner, Peter McCarthy, to support our efforts to get off to a great start.

My role as Lead Proposer for the new school shifted towards co-ordinating strategic aspects of the school, working alongside the ECC Nursery, addressing issues arising from sharing facilities, and securing the permanent site, leaving the day to day running of the school to the team. My role was not funded within the establishment, so at some point during the year, I took on other education consultancy assignments. This included being appointed as a consultant for New Schools Network, which opened opportunities for me to assist other groups interested in setting up schools.

6

PREPARATIONS FOR OUR PERMANENT SITE

MOVE TO PERMANENT SITE ON THE DRIVE

Negotiations to acquire St Mary's old site took a while, and we could not make the school location known until the formal agreement in May 2012.

Moving to the site was contingent on St Mary's decanting to their new premises on Wood Street. There was also some essential refurbishment and upgrade works, previously identified in the government's annual school condition surveys.

The provision of adequate and appropriate school buildings formed part of the pre-opening activities, and, although temporary facilities had been secured at ECC, the project management team proceeded to set the scene for the essential works at The Drive. MACE Group was appointed as construction project manager and KIER as the Principal

Contractor. We appointed Tooley Foster Partnership, the architectural firm who had designed the original St Mary's Junior Infants School buildings back in 1972, and later added the award-winning ARK building.

The contractor and designers produced the scope of works and budget costings. It was necessary to access the site in a timely manner, firm up the contract sum and programme, and deliver the works before the start of the 2013/2014 academic year. The latter point depended on vacant possession.

There were several meetings with the Education Funding Agency (EFA) and DfE about the permanent site, and we hoped to get on site soon, however there were several challenges. Our predecessor had installed temporary classrooms on the playground, and we were told these could not be removed until the summer holiday in 2013. A further worry was their commitment to run summer classes on the premises, which would directly impact on our ability to undertake the works. Moreover, we learnt that St Mary's occupation of the Wood Street site was delayed due to a late discovery of hazardous materials.

There were some fraught exchanges of correspondence with EFA and DfE in the spring of 2013. We were asked to consider a 'Plan B' just in case St Mary's decant programme continued to be a challenge to the ECS relocation. On the other hand, TEST had significant constraints as the temporary accommodation at Erskine Road was inadequate to fit a second cohort for September 2013, nor was there time to seek alternatives.

Eventually, the proposed summer school never took place.

While we awaited the site hand-over, it was agreed that TEST could commence an initial phase of work and store our equipment in an empty classroom, provided we arranged for insurance and supplied St Mary's headteacher with two sets of keys. However, an 'access licence' was required from the Diocese of Chelmsford, the authority in whom the land was vested. The necessary arrangements were made to remove the temporary classrooms and ensure we could start school in September. It was also agreed that the Site manager would give the workers access to the site in the mornings and come back in the evenings to lock up.

A start date of 4th August 2013 was agreed. The workers turned up but were later told to leave the site since they had no 'permission' to be there!

I had a telephone conversation with the project manager from MACE Group, who was on her way to a meeting on site with our ECS team, but she was unable to clarify the issues to me. Although I was not originally scheduled to attend this meeting, I decided to go along.

Once on site, we met in the school reception area, carried out introductions and set the agenda for the day. The Early Years team would look around and agree on the space they needed, while other staff finalised locations for whiteboards and interactive boards within the teaching spaces. As the discussion continued, the Project manager indicated that she needed to speak to me alone.

We walked into another room, where we discussed the refusal of access. She had found out that St. Mary's new site in Wood Street had been ready for well over four weeks, as later confirmed by the Borough official responsible for school moves.

When the EFA representative arrived, he showed me the email he received a few minutes prior from St. Mary's solicitors. The email contained seven very onerous (*I decided there and then not to use the word impossible*) conditions that had to be fulfilled before access to the site was granted. The earliest possible date was 1st of September. I struggled to read through the document a second time, infuriated and frustrated that these conditions were being imposed in a way that could make it impossible to open our doors to students in September.

It was a moment of "*Where do I go from here?*" I couldn't understand why these obstacles would be put in our path at this last minute. I initially started rationalising, and attempted to counter the conditions, but I was helpless in the face of the legal jargon. At this point, I thought it was best not to inform others so that they could carry on without this acutely discouraging news.

The best way forward would be through diplomatic negotiation and prayers. So, I asked Gabriel the EFA rep to speak to the solicitors and get some clarity, while I would contact our solicitor and advocate. I moved into the room next door, spread the pieces of paper on the floor and prayed, citing the story of Hezekiah in 2 Kings 19, when Hezekiah, as king of the embattled state of Judah, placed a threatening letter from his adversary Nebuchadnezzar before God in prayer. I left Gabriel to carry on while I went to our solicitor at Veale Wasbrough Vizards LLP (VWV). Tara McDougall, the MACE project manager was to continue with the meeting in 'business as usual' mode.

As I drove out of the school, I prayed for wisdom on how to tackle this new challenge, considering what was at stake. It was difficult to express the anguish. As I prayed, I thought about the children of Israel crossing the Red Sea; I imagined the scene where some had reached the other side, while the others were still being pursued into the seabed by

Pharaoh's army. With this picture in mind, I recalled that the Israelites all crossed the Red Sea, which encouraged me to believe we would cross to the other side. I was still unsure how to proceed, but by the time I got to Woodford Green, a few minutes later, I resolved to trust God and wait for further instructions.

Wishing there were no more obstacles at this stage, I spent the next two days searching my mind, the Bible, and principles I knew, carefully listening and looking for an answer. *Would God give me a way out?* Finally, I felt a release and sent a CALL TO PRAYER to a few prayer partners.

Responses poured in, as people phoned, emailed, and sent texts to encourage me to hold on. Then, as my husband and I paced up and down the kitchen at our house in Ilford one summer day, discussing the implications of this latest hurdle, he suddenly stopped and said,

"Ade! Let's speak to Ade."

"Get your phone out and speak to him, then." I replied.

"What do we tell him?"

"Give him the facts as they stand, and if nothing else, he can rally prayer support. The least he can do is pray."

As a backdrop, a few days earlier, something 'unusual' had happened. Ade (Pastor Ade Omooba MBE), who had been a great source of encouragement and support, had returned a call which my husband does not remember placing. They had a good catch up about family and the school project. At that time, everything was going well and on time. So, when this impression to call Ade came, it seemed divinely orchestrated. Ade had a scheduled liaison meeting that weekend with the Bishop of Barking and other stakeholders, and he agreed to raise our issues with the site access licence.

The refurbishment programme from Kier Services was phased to ensure that the school term could commence on time in September, therefore, Phase 1 works were scheduled for completion by 28th August 2013. Subsequent phases included the replacement of windows and flat roof finishes to the main building, which were programmed to happen after the start of term. I phoned the MACE project manager for updates daily, even though she promised to get back to me with any news. The countdown was on, and prayers for the school featured on Sunday 11th August at ECC.

On Monday morning 12th August, a fortnight after work should have commenced, I was on my way to Clapham junction in London with a friend, discussing the site saga amongst other things. My phone rang briefly, then disconnected. It was a call from Ade, but I could not respond as we were on the London Underground. Later, during an interview with Impact Teachers, I got a text saying he needed to speak to me urgently. As soon as we stepped out of the interview, I rang Ade who reported favourable news. Miracles had happened that weekend as religious and political leaders met, and the impediments to the access licence for Emmanuel Community School were swept aside. Work could resume on site by 1pm that Monday 12th August!

Following Kier's successful completion of the refurbishment works, we commenced operations in our permanent home.

FIRST OFSTED INSPECTION AFTER OPENING

Our first Ofsted inspection following the opening of the school took place on the 15th and 16th of July 2014. All staff had been informed the previous day of the impending arrival of two inspectors (one was to shadow the other). In preparation, we checked and double checked all our documents, reprinting and replacing some. Staff were in their rooms doing last minute preparations. Various files were piled up ready for scrutiny, reminding me of the pre-opening Ofsted inspection two years earlier. After an 8am site meeting regarding the uncompleted kitchen and a leaking pipe, I met up with the inspectors as Peter, our head teacher took them on a tour of the school. I introduced and excused myself, leaving them to carry on with the site inspection. A few minutes later, Derek came in to inform me that the new boiler was faulty, and there was no guarantee that we would have hot water for the next two days. Health hazard!

This could be a defining moment, I thought. *Do we have any disposable plates and cutlery? Do we have enough? Managing lunch time would be quite challenging without them!* I was scheduled to meet the inspectors at 10:45am, but after checking through the PTA cupboard and kitchen, I decided to head out to Costco, a large, members only warehouse nearby. Jane gave me a list and I left school at 10:00am, praying for clear roads and for me to find the needed items. Both prayers were answered as I dashed across different aisles looking for disposable plates, bowls, and cutlery; and I managed to get back to school just in time for my meeting with the inspectors. By far the fastest shopping trip I have ever done!

The rest of the day seemed to go to plan, except for regular requests for documentation which thankfully were accessible or easily generated. Lauraine had to download some required documents from Dropbox to give to the inspectors. After the inspectors left, we checked that the staff were ok and ready for the next day (as the inspection was for two days). We went over the preliminary feedback and ascertained that we had all the documents requested for the following day and more. Compared to the previous day, we had an early night, leaving school at about 8pm!

Wednesday started as early as the first day, with the inspectors listening to the choir as they practiced. They were quite impressed with the cheerfulness with which staff and volunteers worked. Mrs. Lewis' hearty singing as she helped set out activities in the reception outdoor play area was a bonus. The inspectors looked through students' books and folders, then met with Trust directors, parents, and students. They listened to students read, observed lessons, interviewed almost every adult in the school and looked through every child's book. We had a final feedback meeting around 4pm but had to wait for the official feedback sometime later. (*See next section*).

The rest of the school term passed swiftly, and the school broke up later in July for a well-earned summer break.

PART TWO

WHAT IT WAS LIKE IN SCHOOL – FROM THE VIEWPOINT OF OUR FIRST COHORT OF CHILDREN

This section was compiled from the weekly school newsletters issued to children and parents during each of the school years 2012 – 2019, with added commentary to provide clarity or context.

7

OPERATING FROM OUR PERMANENT PREMISES

We started our second year in September 2013 on our new and permanent school site, with two classes: Reception and Year 1. We were now, officially, Emmanuel Community School, The Drive, Walthamstow E17 3BN, in London Borough of Waltham Forest. Comparing the new site to our temporary premises, our children commented, "this school is very big with lots of space to run around, with a climbing frame and a pirate ship". More children and adults joined our school, and some of the adults now had new roles:

Ms. Dyer – Reception Class Teacher & Early Years Foundation Stage Leader

Ms. Mwaura – Reception Teaching Assistant

Ms. Thomas – Year 1 Class Teacher

Ms. Davis – Year 1 Teaching Assistant

Ms. Spence – Special Educational Needs Co-ordinator & Inclusion Leader

Mrs. Jackson – Community Liaison Officer & Cover Teacher

Mr. Bown – School Keeper

Ms. Owusu-Ansah – School Cleaner

Ms. Cristofoli – Volunteer

Ms. Hyatt and Ms. Perkins – YMCA breakfast and after school club.

Our initial governing board consisted of:

- Rev Anthony Hodgkinson (Chair of Governors)
- Mrs. Titilayo Oluwatudimu (Lead Proposer)
- Peter Lewis (Head Teacher)
- Dr Akin Oluwatudimu (Governor and Premises/PM Lead)
- Hilda Jackson (Staff Governor)
- Rev Doug Williams (Vice-Chair)
- Richard Irish (Governor and Finance Lead)
- Lauraine Colthart (Governor and Marketing Lead)
- Bentley Greaves (Governor and IT Lead)
- Natasha Alvis and Deborah Richards (Parent Governors).

At the end of the first week, Reception class won the first attendance trophy. It was great fun having a fire engine and fire fighters in our school on 19th September. The reception class students were allowed to play in the fire engine. And our first non-uniform day was the next day. We learned about genetic disorders and donated £1.00 each to the charity *Jeans for Genes*. There was also a great turn out of parents for our Harvest festival on 27th September, and all the items were donated to the *180 Homeless Project*. Several parents came to walk around the school premises on Thursday 3rd October.

Gordon and Amanda (parents) had worked hard to set up the Parent and Teacher Association (PTA). On Friday 18th October, they met with several parents and grandparents to plan interesting activities, one of which was an International Food Extravaganza to celebrate the diverse ethnicities in the school population. They organized this on the 25th of October, after school in the main hall. There were dishes from so many parts of the world. We tasted food from several countries, including fried plantain, jollof rice, salt fish with green bananas, salt fish cakes, tortillas, samosas, apple pies and lots more. We also learned about the different cultures represented in our school. Some parents dressed in traditional clothing and came into classes to talk about ethnic foods and the origins of their outfits. They also shared folktales in English and in their mother tongues.

It was phonics and reading training for all Reception (Hedgehogs) and Year One (Squirrels) parents on 25th October. The classes were initially allocated animal names to provide a connection to nature. This was later changed to reflect the colours of the rainbow, which was deemed more appropriate.

Emmanuel Community School became a centre of support for the community. One of the Local Authority's Early Intervention (EI) teams moved into the empty classrooms behind the school hall. Children were not allowed into this area, which became known as the school's adult section. Parents needing help with housing, legal issues or other assistance could get the support they needed onsite (while school continued), through the collaborative work between TEST and the Local Authority. As such, the EI Team was able to occupy the premises rent-free.

Extra-curricular activities kicked off in this new term with Mr. Lewis's choir on Wednesdays at 8:15am and achievement awards assembly from 3:00-3:20pm.

As a free school, the Department for Education was monitoring our progress, so on the 5th of November 2013, DfE advisers Sue Phillips and Debbie Coslett spent the day with us. They examined different aspects of the school and had many positive things to say. They even remarked, "the children are lovely."

Children were given holiday diaries assignments to keep a diary of their half-term week off, to include photos, writing, drawings, event tickets, tube tickets, postcards, etc. After the half term break, Mrs. Gurman started a lunchtime art club on Mondays for Year 1 and Wednesdays for Reception.

We had great fun when the Blunderbus Theatre Company visited to present '*How to Catch a Star*', based on the picture book by Oliver Jeffers. We also started collecting and filling shoe boxes for Operation Christmas Child, and the boxes were collected in November.

Next, we elected a boy and a girl from each class to our student council. Each student standing for election presented a one-minute speech to their class on Monday 4th November, after which we voted. Our first elected student council members were Aston and Alissa in Reception, Nazareth and Nathan in Year 1. They had their first meeting and posted the minutes on the student council notice board in the school hall, which is centrally located, easily accessed from all the classes. It is also the hub for group activities, assemblies, drama, and music events, as well as the dining room. The council's first task was to organize

Pyjama Day to raise funds for Children in Need on the 15th of November.

Christmas season began with a fantastic Christmas party, organized by our new PTA team on the 14th of December. Equally fantastic was the nativity play by our Year 1 class on the 18th of December. The term ended with a Christmas carol service the following day, with lots of real candles lit around the school hall. We were then off on holiday till the 6th of January 2014.

8

3RD YEAR 2014/2015

After the summer break, we came back in September 2014 to our third year, with more students, including a new reception class and new staff. Ms. Harley was in Year 1, Mrs. Greaves and Mr. Olokun also joined the staff team. Year 2 (the first Yellow Class) had Ms. James as the teacher.

The school office, which was previously directly off the street (in the part of the school we call the Ark), was relocated to the main building next to the Headteacher's office. The Ark was an extension to the main building and has a curved shape and timber cladding which reminds us of Noah's ark in the Bible.

Our class names were changed from animals to colours of the rainbow to remind us of God's covenant. Reception became known as RED, Year 1 - ORANGE, Year 2 – YELLOW. The rest of the colours of the rainbow were allocated for subsequent years, Year 3 - GREEN, Year 4 -

BLUE, Year 5 - INDIGO, and Year 6 – VIOLET. We started swimming and recorder lessons. The PTA offered coffee mornings in the Ark throughout the week of 8th September from 9:15am – 11:15am to provide networking opportunities and support for parents, while the reception students had a staggered start with their first full school day on the following Monday.

Following the inspection in July, we finally received the published Ofsted report in September 2014, with a news feature in the local Guardian on the 23rd of September. The report showed that the school had come a long way in a short time, and we were delighted with the positive comments. It was great to read that we were judged to be a good school with outstanding features. This extract was put on our website:

> *"Having opened as a new school in September 2012, our first ever Ofsted report is extremely encouraging. The report shows the school to be good with outstanding features and that outstanding leadership has led to establishing a good school within a short time. We are excited about building on this strong foundation as we seek to move to outstanding in all areas.*

Comments from the report include:

- *Outstanding leadership by the headteacher, leaders and governors has established a good school within a short time.*
- *Pupils make good progress.*
- *Teaching is good because staff have high expectations.*
- *Provision for pupils' spiritual, moral, social, and cultural development is excellent. It is embedded in the subjects taught and in the ethos of the school.*
- *The school's work to keep pupils safe and secure is outstanding.*
- *The school is a caring and nurturing place in which pupils behave well and get on well with each other. Pupils and adults care for and respect each other.*
- *The headteacher and the governing body are very ambitious for the school and have secured sustainable improvements in teaching and achievement over the last two years.*
- *The senior team of the headteacher, Early Years Foundation Stage Leader, and the Trust*

Director of Education work especially well together.

- *The school is supported very ably by the governing body, which plays a crucial role in leading the strategic overview.*

The report also states: There is a clear vision for further improvement and a strong determination to bring this about.

We are delighted that our report includes this comment, because it reflects the aim of our whole school community to move the school forward to be the best it can be for our pupils and families.

We are grateful to our parents, carers and pupils who took the time to speak to inspectors during the inspection. It is fantastic to read on the Ofsted Parent View Survey that 100% of respondents would 'recommend our school to another parent'.

We have outstanding children at our school, and we are very proud of them. They can be pleased to read Ofsted's report and to know that their excellent approach to school has been acknowledged. With such fantastic children and a strong school community we know that, by God's grace, Emmanuel Community School will go from strength to strength."

We had a Free School Meals celebration on Thursday 2nd October. Our catering staff put on a special menu with samples showing how yummy school meals can be. We also learnt that the government had decided that school meals are now free for all infant pupils.

On Saturday, 10th of October, our governors spent the day planning how to improve our school.

During our Harvest Festival, we raised £40.20 for the New Hope Trust, a charity supporting the homeless, while all food donations were sent to the local night shelter project. Tina (aka Mrs Longhurst) baked very beautiful bread for the occasion. We also had a Harvest colouring competition. The winning entries were Georgie from Red class, with Israel as a runner up; Frankie from Orange class, and Joella from Yellow class. The adult winners were Lionel and Lorelle.

Mrs. Oluwatudimu, the lead proposer for our school met the Prime Minister, Rt. Hon. David Cameron MP and the new Secretary of State for Education, Rt. Hon. Nicky Morgan MP at a reception organized by the New Schools Network (NSN) for free school openers on 15th October. A Reading and Phonics Workshop for our Parents was held shortly after, and our 2014 Macmillan Coffee Day raised £162.61!

Yellow class travelled to the National Portrait Gallery on the 20th of October, and parents came into school to celebrate Black History month on Thursday 23rd and again on Friday to discuss their children's progress with teachers before we left on half-term.

On 11th November, we remembered the people that fought to protect the place we call home. This was part of the Armistice Remembrance Day Celebration which marks the end of the 1st World War. As part of other charity activities, we filled 32 boxes for the shoe box appeal and wore Pyjamas to school on Friday 14th November for a £1 donation in aid of Children in Need. We started December with visits to St Mary's Church, Walthamstow, to experience the Christmas story. Red class went on Monday 1st, Orange class the next day and Yellow class on the 3rd.

Our PTA organized several events. Amanda, Angela, and Sarah as part of the PTA, did a great job in getting lots of parents and family friends to the quiz night where they had a fish and chips dinner. The event raised £340.07. They funded the Blunderbus Theatre Company's performance of *I've Seen Santa* on 4th December. They also organized the production of a tea towel design with our portraits on them. This was displayed on the parents' notice board in the playground. We were able to give them to family and friends as Christmas gifts.

The last few days of the term were busy with different Christmas activities. One of the most exciting events was the children's Christmas party held on 5th December. We brought in our party clothes in the morning, so we could change after school. No parents or siblings were allowed to join in. We had party food and got Christmas presents. We had a special guest – Father Christmas! - who gave us all presents. A special grotto was constructed where we listened to the Christmas story. Children from a nearby nursery school also visited the grotto to hear the Christmas story, while staff and governors had their Christmas meal at a restaurant on Lea Bridge Road the following week.

Red class performed *Carols in the Classroom* to parents, who then had an opportunity to look at the work the children had done during the term. They were encouraged to complete colourful stickers to commend good performance known as 'WOW' slips to go into the children's folders. Yellow class put on a wonderful performance of *Jesus is the Reason for the Season* on Wednesday 17th December, to a packed-out hall of parents, grandparents, and other family members. This was our third and last time of presenting the nativity play, as we would be in the Junior classes next year, so the year below would be doing this.

Those of us who attended Trekkers & Champions (Emmanuel Community Church's weekly outreach activity club for primary-aged children that took place at our school) also had a Christmas Party on Thursday 18th December from 6:00 to 7:45pm. The term ended with a Candlelit Carol service on 19th December 2014, for which the school hall was again filled to capacity.

SPRING TERM 2015

Spring term started on Tuesday 6th January 2015 with Mrs. Jackson's attendance slogan – **"On time is good, early is best**!!!" on posters all over the school.

Two student teachers from the University of East London worked in Orange and Yellow classes this term. Several clubs, including Drama, PE, Maths and Music, started in the week of 12th January, some for specific groups, such as the Art club for Year 1, while the Spanish club was for children and parents. It was great fun to learn new words, play games and sing songs during this club.

Young Writers published stories from fourteen of us in year 2, in a book titled, ***Once Upon a Time – Amazing Tales.*** We read out some of these stories in assembly, and many parents bought copies of the book. We felt this was a major achievement.

On 30th January, we said goodbye to Mrs. Lee, our midday supervisor, who went to look after her new grandchild. She had started the awards for good manners and behaviour in the dining room. She played special music during lunch and made us think of the dining hall as a special restaurant.

We had the Good Samaritan colouring competition in February. The winners were: Marceau and Tanscelle in Red Class; Kevin and Adrian in Orange Class; Nuria and Joella in Yellow Class. Aston was also recognised for his effort. 'Election Fever' was upon us as we selected our new school council representatives on the 13th of February.

On 2nd March, the school governors spent the day listening to us read and taking part in class activities. World Book Day on 21st March was a fantastic celebration as staff and students dressed up as book characters. It was great to guess who they were and to read their stories.

As part of their 'Around the World' topic, Red class thoroughly enjoyed creating a Eurostar train in their classroom and simulating a visit to Paris. Their 'passports' were stamped at the model 'Departure Lounge' as they came in with their 'hand luggage'. Then we took part in the Children's Food Trust's "Big Cookathon 2015", on Friday 6th March. We were given the recipes beforehand, so we practiced making the dishes at home over the half term.

We participated in a sponsored '*Readathon*'; a great chance to read more fantastic books at home. From 12th-18th March we held a Scholastic book fair for half an hour before and after school. Everyone had a £1 book token to spend during this week.

Our fantastic Year 1, Orange Class, gave a wonderful performance of an Easter musical, *Here Comes Jesus!* on Monday 30th March. As part of our RE lessons and Easter celebrations, we visited St. Mary's Church of England, Walthamstow, to participate in their Easter activities. We also wore our homemade Easter hats and bonnets to school on Wednesday 1st April and enjoyed having a Parade during assembly.

A few new things introduced this term included the lovely scooter shed in the reception play area, so, more children brought scooters to school. The Bible Society made their free children's Bible Story App available to us, encouraging parents to read the Easter story at home. We could also read more stories over the Easter break by logging on to the school website.

The Early Help Service (also known as the Early Intervention and Prevention Team) who shared our building, provided a 'Schools Open programme' during the Easter break for children aged from 5-11 years who lived within the Borough, whether they attended our school or not. This ran from 7th – 17th April 2015. It was a first for Emmanuel Community School and the holiday programme was free to families, while meals were subsidised. Mrs. Jackson and Mrs. Oluwatudimu coordinated the activities. The day started with fun activities, then a fruit break, followed by numeracy activities before lunch and more great games afterwards. We also went on trips, including visiting the City Farm in Leyton.

Our link church, Emmanuel Christian Centre (subsequently renamed Emmanuel Community Church International) celebrated its centenary with services on Good Friday and Easter Sunday at Walthamstow Academy, Billet Road, Walthamstow E17.

SUMMER TERM 2015

Our school nurse started providing a weekly drop-in service for parents to discuss health concerns. Orange class started swimming lessons on Tuesday 21st April, and for St. George's Day on the 23rd, we were allowed to wear red and white. We had another International Food Extravaganza after school on Friday 1st of May to celebrate students and staff ethnic diversity, and share food from various parts of the world.

School was closed on the 7th of May because our premises was used as a polling station. After the elections, we used the polling booths for our very own election practice on the 11th of May. When the votes came in, we had selected Katy the Pony, with 32 votes, as our adopted animal. The school council also organised a Tabletop Sale on the 8th of May.

During half term, Orange class had a sleepover in school! We came to school with our sleeping bags and pyjamas, had great games, decorated cupcakes, had dinner, listened to stories, watched movies, and then went off to bed, or rather, off to sleep on beddings laid on the floor. The adults, our teachers and Mr. Lewis, were great at cooking, playing games and giving us a great time.

Activities that started this term included sports coaching by Tottenham Hotspur Foundation. We also started preparing for the carnival and Summer Fayre. The summer fayre boards went up outside houses around the school and the local area. When the day arrived on 18th June, the PTA put on a great event for families tagged "The Love E17 Festival of Culture". We had puppet shows, a live band, lots of food and drinks; but most importantly it was a great family day out. The choir and the gymnastic group also performed, and we raised an impressive £1500!

This funding went towards inspiring, educational activities to support the school and enrich our community, such as:

- An entire school Theatre trip to Hackney Empire for the Christmas pantomime – Jack and The Beanstalk.
- READATHON Competition prizes to encourage a love of reading.
- School equipment and visitors' refreshments for the Queen's Birthday celebrations.
- Contributions towards books and materials for the library.
- Awards for children and teachers who completed the Hackney Schools Half Marathon.
- Sports Day refreshments.

> Our headteacher noted that: *"The Tottenham Hotspur Foundation has provided high quality coaching for all of our pupils as part of their work in our community. Children have really enjoyed the fun, focused and purposeful activities."*

The Watoto Children's Choir from Uganda stopped by at Emmanuel Community School on 3rd July 2015, during their tour of Europe. Accompanied by a team of adults, the choir presented the Watoto charity's vision and mission through their stories, music, and dance, acting as ambassadors to raise awareness about the plight of the orphaned and vulnerable children of Uganda. For their special performance at Emmanuel, each member of the choir was given their very own Spurs outfit in the team colours, courtesy of Tottenham Hotspur Foundation.

Emmanuel Community School took part in the Waltham Forest Carnival for the first time on Sunday 5th of July. We danced along Leyton High Street in costumes (made in our workshops with the help of some parents and teachers). The audience along the road cheered us on, and we had our photographs taken.

The school community was informed that The Emmanuel School Trust (TEST), the trust responsible for our school, was preparing a proposal to open a second school in the borough. An application would be made to the government, so they issued a questionnaire and online survey to be completed by parents and anyone who was interested.

Red class enjoyed their pirate-themed activities, with pirate ships and costumes around the school as they learnt about pirates. They also had another fascinating activity involving incubating fertilised chick and duck eggs in their classroom. There was such great excitement as the eggs hatched 21 days later, and the chicks emerged. This event was recorded on video – thanks to Mrs. Colthart – amid squeals of delight. The class enjoyed looking after and writing about the chicks. Sadly, they had to say goodbye once the chicks got too big for the classroom and moved to their new home at Brooks Farm in Leyton. Goodbye chicks!

Monday 13th July was our transition day when prospective reception students and their parents visited the school. The students met their prospective class teachers and classmates, while parents had a transition meeting in the hall to discuss the school vision, attendance, and attainment in preparation for the start of term in September 2015.

At the end of the term in July, we said goodbye to Mrs Gurman and Miss Morris, both of whom had been with us since the school opened.

SUMMER HOLIDAYS 2015

During the summer holidays, staff and volunteers from our school and from The Emmanuel School Trust participated in community events within Waltham Forest, to raise awareness about our school and the proposed second free school. There was a stall at the Waltham Forest MELA event at Chestnuts Playing fields. We had a clown (Mrs. Jackson), and staff and volunteers provided free face painting and balloons. It was a great opportunity to interact with different families in the community and to publicise Emmanuel Community School. A few weeks later, on 15th of August, the team were again in action with another community event in Chingford, north of the borough.

9

4TH YEAR 2015/2016

SEPTEMBER 2015

At the start of the autumn term, our teachers had a full day of training, while the children had an extra day at home. There were some changes to the start and end of our school day to make it safer and easier for parents to drop and pick us up. By now, we were in Green class with Ms. Harley as our teacher.

"Early is best, on time is good, but late is not an option" was the attendance mantra for this year.

Children with 100% attendance had their names put into a hat and, at the end of the term, a boy and a girl were awarded a scooter. All other children with 100% received a badge and certificate.

Every week, we have an assembly dedicated to highlighting and celebrating remarkable and outstanding achievements, referred to as the awards or celebration assembly. This term, this activity was moved to Fridays from 2:55pm – 3:15pm in the school hall.

We collected donations of clothes, food, and toiletries for the harvest festival. Prospective parents visited the premises between September and December 2015. Our head teacher would usually bring them to our class and tell them that we were the oldest children in the school.

Parents within the community were offered free 13-week Parenting Classes, to develop parenting skills and help increase self-esteem and confidence. This term, the Parenting Classes focused on the theme, 'Strengthening Families, Strengthening Communities', and were held weekly on Tuesdays from 6th October-19th January from 9:30am to 12:30pm. The classes covered topics like special time; causes of behaviour and praise.

WORLD CUP RUGBY SCHOOL DINNER MENU – WEDNESDAY 23RD SEPTEMBER

To celebrate the World Cup Rugby tournament, which started on Friday 18th September, our cook served a special menu consisting of Spicy Chicken "Wingers", "Haka" Pizza, "Rucking" Potato wedges, "Drop Goal" sweetcorn, "Line Out" Peas, "Scrummy" Toffee Cream Tart, Chocolate "Rugby Ball", Shortbread Biscuits, and "Knock

On" Fresh Fruit Platter. This was a great way to join in the fun.

Children in Need was great fun; we collected coins and had a "Great Coin Race". Over sixty of us attended the Children in Need disco as part of our fund-raising events, and our **Champions of Change were featured on national television as part of the BBC's *Children in Need* programme.** It was exciting to be part of a national initiative such as this, and staff and parents were also thrilled that our fund-raising was acknowledged on television. This was a great achievement for a new school like ours, which only started in 2012, considering how many schools there are in this country.

As usual, every year, the school arranges for professional photographs of all children to be taken. The photographer set up in the school hall, which is the largest space, and we had to line up and take photographs with the whole class and our teachers. We also took photographs with our siblings.

We sent congratulatory messages to Mrs Mwaura on the arrival of her baby boy.

The PTA organised a wonderful Christmas Bazaar on Saturday 5th December 2015 from 1:00pm to 4:00pm. They raised £847.23, which was added to the £1500 raised during the summer fayre.

During the last few days of the term, we had lots of Christmas activities. This included Yellow class's Nativity performance on Wednesday 16th, class parties on Thursday, and the school term finished with a Candlelit Carol Service on Friday. Then over the weekend, some students and staff joined our link church, Emmanuel Community Church International, for a celebration of Christmas on Sunday 20th.

SPRING TERM 2016

We started the new term on the 5th of January and settled into our learning with very interesting topics. The whole school went on a sponsored march for Health Poverty Action, 'STOMP', on 12th February, to raise awareness and funds for children who live without water. We pretended to stamp out poverty and inequality. Many parents joined us in the march to Walthamstow Central and back. It was a very cold day, so we wore our wellies and funny hats, and enjoyed leading chants and songs as cars stopped to let us cross and other people joined the march as we went past. We raised a massive £452.50 to help make positive changes for the people affected by poverty whom we had learnt about from our lessons.

We had a book fair. The school bought more books, so children could choose their favourites. World Book Day was all about characters from Roald Dahl's books. Science Week was also great – each class had a different theme. The last day was the greatest as many parents joined in our fantastic experiments. They enjoyed the lessons so much that they wanted to stay on in school after the session had ended!

Along with the amazing performance of *Resurrection Rocks* by Green Class with Ms. Harley, we had a violin performance, and our annual Easter Bonnet parade as part of the end of term activities. We were set the Readathon competition for the holidays.

As Easter approached, we learnt a lot about the events of the season, including that Easter eggs are hollow to symbolise the 'tomb' being empty. We wrote acronyms for Easter. Here is one example:

> **E** – **E**aster is reminding Christians of when Jesus was on the Cross.
>
> **A** – **A**n Easter egg reminds us of when Jesus was in the tomb.
>
> **S** – **S**oon, Jesus came out of the tomb and back to life.
>
> **T** – **T**he Last Supper, Jesus said to the disciples, 'Take this and eat it, it's my Body'.

E – **E**aster gives the children an Easter egg and there's nothing in it.

R – **R**esurrection, Jesus rose again.

At the celebration assembly to round up the term, various awards were given out. Another set of happy scooter owners was announced, because they had been in school every day in the last term! We said goodbye to Miss Davis but welcomed Mr. Bowen (our Site Supervisor since we moved to The Drive) into a new role as a teaching assistant.

This term, our morning and after school activities were branded as 'Rise and Shine' club. This was a wrap-around provision so working parents could bring children to school before normal school hours, and benefit from activities and supervision after school. However, unlike last year, we did not have the 'Schools Open programme' or Easter holiday Club.

SUMMER TERM 2016

Summer Term started on the 12th of April, with great anticipation of celebrating the Queen's birthday. We also heard the news of the wedding of Ms Dyer, one of our teachers who had become Mrs. Grace. To promote good health and wellbeing of students, Emmanuel Community School signed up to the government's Healthy Schools initiative. Schools can gain gold, silver or bronze certificates to display in schools, and children are encouraged to share their success with parents. Most of us received '*Eggsellent*' skipping ropes as Easter gifts from school, since '*Skipness 4 Fitness*' was our focus as part of our Silver Healthy Schools Award this term.

We had a week-long Queen's 90th birthday celebration, and some of our school's activities were featured in the Waltham Forest Guardian newspaper, which made us very proud. We also had a Queen's Portrait competition with a record number of amazing entries by the children, which were displayed in the portrait gallery. Samuel won the competition. We rounded up the week with a picnic, and many senior citizens from the community joined us for the day.

Another initiative promoting good health was the annual Hackney Schools' Challenge, which took place at the Queen Elizabeth Olympic Park and is open to school children from Hackney and neighbouring boroughs. It is sponsored by some big companies. Many of our children took part on Sunday 10th May and completed our first ever half Marathon run. We practised running around our school playground for many weeks in preparation for this event and, on the day, we were some of the youngest participants. Our teachers told us we made them very proud.

There was great excitement in Red, Orange and Yellow classes as they watched how things grow in their classes. They had 15 chrysalises and on 13th May, they had their first three butterflies. Orange class then created gardens for homework, which was judged by the school governors. As of 19th May, Red class had 8 chicks and 2 butterflies, which generated much interest around the school.

The summer fayre this year had a colourful celebration feel to it – **Love E17: Festival of Culture**. (E17 is the post code for Walthamstow, where the school is located). Despite the weather, we had a fantastic turn out, raising a record-breaking £2,250.

Pastor Anthony Hodgkinson, the Chair of Governors wrote to the school. Below is an excerpt from his message:

"*Dear Emmanuel Community School,*

Big crowds, big pockets, big hearts, beautiful day, incredible creativity, diversity and everyone left with hearts aglow. It is great to know we raised significant funds. However, our Christian school is a COMMUNITY school. On that count, we outdid ourselves! The spirit and demeanour in which everyone worked together was admirable.

Big thank you to PTA, their families, (who lost them for a whole day) stall holders, organisers, volunteers, cheerleaders who excite everyone with vision, the staff, and every other member of the school community who came along and made the day so perfect.

A big thanks to God from whom ALL blessings flow–without Him all of this would not only be impossible, but it would also have no purpose. On behalf of the leaders at ECCI and the whole of our glorious GB – ***THANK YOU SO MUCH for supporting this wonderful event.***"

The **LOVE E17** event was also attended by the Mayor of Waltham Forest. We are grateful that our mayors attend special events at ECS. We received the following note from the Mayor:

> *"I was delighted to be able to share part of Emmanuel's LOVE E17: Festival of Culture. Although I was there for just a short while, I could feel the warmth and enthusiasm of everyone involved. I was impressed with the hard work that had gone into the day, and I hope it becomes a regular feature in the school's calendar."*
>
> *Mayor of Waltham Forest Cllr Peter Herrington*

The funds raised at LOVE E17 enriched and supported the school community through the provision of items including a basketball hoop, sand pit for outdoor activities, seeds for "Edible Garden project", refreshments during sports day, and the purchase of trophies. This year the PTA nominated the East London Pearly Queens & Kings Society, which supports a range of charities, to receive a donation. The society will use the donation to support The Children's Trust, Alzheimer's Society, Dream Factory and Diabetes UK.

On 27th May, we took part in 'Education Sunday' Service at Emmanuel Community Church at Walthamstow Academy, where we acted out our school values. Education Sunday is an annual event held by churches in the UK on the second Sunday in September. It is a nationwide day of prayer for everyone involved in any aspect of education, from students to employees. English and Welsh churches have been observing Education Sunday for over a century. Later, we said farewell to Ms. Waugh who left us on Thursday 30th June.

We were not left out of the football fever for Euro 2016, which took place in France from 10th June to 10th July. We had a map of the world and a table of the competing teams in the hall and completed the league tables as the teams played the matches. We even had a football themed menu on Friday 24th June. It was good to follow such an important and international tournament, with some healthy rivalry regarding the teams representing the countries we supported (The ECS community includes students and staff from many countries).

ECS children also took part in the annual Waltham Forest Carnival, for which this year's theme was 'Creatures Great and Small'. We really enjoyed participating in this event that celebrates and appreciates the ethnic diversity in the borough.

We had a whole school trip to the Olympic Park on 8th July, where we staged our very own mini-Olympics at the venue, in preparation for the 2016 Rio de Janeiro Olympics. We had a fantastic end of the school year with events and class parties, a music concert, violin and recorder performances and the school choir singing. Sports Day was on 12th July at Lloyd Park. It was a great success until we experienced heavy rain during lunch and the rest of the activities had to be postponed. We had to return to school, and only completed our Sports Day on Tuesday 19th July, with trophy presentations to the winning team in a special assembly. There were also prizes for children who scored 100% attendance.

As the weather was now warmer, we enjoyed 'Ice Cream Friday' after a PTA stand appeared in the playground with ice lollies and creams for sale. It was a great way to get rewarded at the end of the week.

ECS HIGHLIGHTS 2015-2016

The children at ECS have really enjoyed the activities they participated in this year. Here are some we highlighted:

Jack and the Beanstalk pantomime (Hackney Empire)

Christmas Nativity - Sleepy Shepherd

Excellent teaching

Help with reading

Maths lessons

Science Week

Easter Bonnet Parade

Easter Musical - Resurrection Rock

Half Marathon

Summer Fayre

Party in the Class

Sports Day

Olympic Park Visit & mini-Olympic competition

10

5TH YEAR 2016/2017

SEPTEMBER 2016

The autumn term of this academic year started with the arrival of another set of Red class (reception) children and their parents. The new parents were invited for coffee and cookies on Wednesday 5th September at 9:30am. Some of the new things this year included "Memory Verse Thursday". We started learning a verse from the Bible every week in assembly, and a written reminder was included in the regular newsletter which was sent out to parents.

The first cohort were now in Blue class with Mr. Lazarus. The cost of school dinners for Year 3 and Year 4 increased from £2.00 to £2.10 and the school launched 'Parent Pay', an online electronic payment platform for school dinners and other things. We did not need to take our brown money envelopes to the school office anymore.

The PTA – Parents and Teachers Association – changed its name to PTFA – Parents, Teachers and Friends Association – to represent the growing support received from the school, neighbourhood and church communities. This year they focused on awareness, inclusion and empowering.

Our Harvest festival in September was themed 'Bread of Life for life', and the proceeds were donated to support the Waltham Forest Night Shelter.

The school community received the good news that an application to the Department of Education by The Emmanuel Community School Trust (TEST), to open a second Christian Primary school, had been successful. A new two-form entry school, proposed within the Waltham Forest borough, was endorsed to progress into what was described as the 'pre-opening' phase by the Department for Education.

In the meantime, the focus was to work "From Good to Outstanding" in every area of our school, especially in our behaviour for learning. To assist with achieving this, we had Tracey Campbell, a behaviour consultant observing us in the playground and working with some parents. We also had Ruth Coles, a Speech and Language Therapist working with some teachers.

Orange Class went on a 'Build a Bear' trip to Westfield Stratford on 5th October. They had a splendid time and returned to school with two additional members to their class (the carefully named Peanut Butter and Sunshine) who would be going home with a child from Orange class each weekend.

For Dyslexic Awareness Week (3rd -7th October), we had several activities including a visit from Marcia Brissett-Bailey of the Waltham Forest Dyslexia Association. She gave a very informative talk and hosted an information session for all parents and carers on "What's it like to have Dyslexia?" Every child in the room received a goody bag which helped us understand dyslexia better. Our new look Emmanuel Community School Library opened on the Thursday with Dyslexia-friendly books.

Our first morning prayer gathering took place on Tuesday 4th October from 8:15 – 8:45am with students, parents, carers and teachers joining in. It later became known as 'Prayer Space' and was initially held every second Tuesday of the month.

We had a fantastic Diversity Week celebrating our differences and similarities in October, with parents and grandparents coming to share their wonderful stories and read to us from various cultures. We were provided with a list of books to enjoy at home. These included:

- *I am an Artist* by Marta Altos
- *Splash Anna Hibiscus* by Atinuke & Lauren Tobia
- *Ada Twist Scientist* by Andrea Beaty
- *My Two Grannies* by Floella Benjamin and
- *Of Thee I Sing – A letter to my daughters* by Barack Obama.

We also enjoyed a delicious Black History Month menu, had a poetry/poster competition, and the week ended with the Mbilla Drumming Performance to our parents in the school hall.

School Counsellors were elected on Tuesday 17th October with Orange Class - Hugo and Imogen, Yellow Class - Israel and Jia Ming, Green Class - Shaun and Iliana, and Blue Class - Nicholas and Riah.

We had a Superheroes and Friends Disco Party on Friday 18th November at 6pm for Children in Need. The terrific Trekkers team helped to host the party. There were exciting glo-stick games, cookies, treats, prizes, dancing and surprise goodie bags! At the end of the event, Emmanuel Community School raised £600 for Children in Need. Some of us travelled to the BBC Studios in London to represent the school at the BBC *Children in Need* programme on television with Mr. Olokun and Mrs. Jackson, while everyone else watched the live broadcast during the Superheroes and Friends Party. This was remarkable and significant for our school, and great publicity, given that our fundraising contribution was featured the year before.

Our teachers encouraged us to read as many books as possible and we were provided with access to an online portal called Oxford Owl, from the Oxford University Press. The Oxford Owl logo was thereafter applied to all our school bags and as stickers on our reading books. We each had an Oxford Owl login and a reading record to access a wide range of exciting books and fun activities which help with learning and development.

Elisabeth Abbott visited us on the 1st and 2nd December with her guide dog, to raise awareness about sight loss and the practical care the Royal National Institute of Blind People (RNIB) offers. Theatre Bugs brought us a Christmas Pantomime, *The Missing Stockings!*, packed with music, laughter, and songs as we helped Goldilocks, Little Red and the Gingerbread Man find their Christmas stockings. We also made self-portrait tea towels with our drawings, which were sold to our families.

On Christmas Jumper Day, Friday 16th, we found out more about the "serious side to all the silliness". Our colourful jumpers were to raise funds to help save children's lives. Our funds would bring healthcare, education, protection, and food to millions of children around the world. We also got a special sticker and balloon!

At the end of the term, we said goodbye to Mrs. Grace who went on maternity leave and welcomed Mrs. Tinuoye to Red Class and Dr Lawson as our Inclusion leader.

Our Christmas activities this year included visits to St. Mary's Church, a Nativity play by Yellow class, carols in the classroom by Red (Reception) class, and a whole school carol service on the last day of school for 2016. All these have now become school traditions.

JANUARY 2017

We came back to school on 3rd January 2017 to start the autumn term after a lovely Christmas break. Our parents were given a list of things we would be doing in our classes and how they could help us. Red Class started the topic 'Off to the Moon'; looking at aliens and reading fun stories to inspire the imagination, learning about stars, planets, and comets with Mrs. Tinuoye. Orange Class started investigating and experimenting on electricity with Miss Ni'Dhughaill. Yellow Class worked on Push and Pulls; Green Fingers went outside to plant some bulbs in the school garden with Mrs. Owen-Reilly. Green Class learned about the Active Planet – how the Earth is formed; what a volcano island is and where they are in the world; what causes an earthquake, and how earthquakes can be measured – with Miss Harley. In Blue Class, we learned about Land, Sea, and Sky, and read the book 'Narnia' by C.S Lewis with Mr. Lazarus.

Boxes with increased storage capacity were installed in the playground, so we had more equipment to play with during break times. We also had a range of creative classroom activities for the Chinese New Year.

Aleksandra, Inas, Jake, Kaylen, Kevin, Khianu, Lauryn, Louda, Nazareth, Nicholas, Riah and Sam demonstrated fantastic sportsmanship at the Peter May Centre, with the support of many parents and staff on 26th January, when we ranked 17th place out of 26 schools in our very first participation in the Borough Sports Athletics Competition. During the assembly on Friday January 27th, we performed some songs from the Young Voices performance at the O2 venue from the night before.

We had a few visitors who worked with us on various topics: Paul Berry came to talk to us about the Passover which relates to our topic about Judaism in RE. Pip Jones, a Children's author visited as part of the World Book Day activities. Jessica from Health Poverty Action came to tell us about the great big *School Stomp*! just like last year, when parents joined in as the entire school stomped down to Walthamstow Market, singing and waving flags to raise funds for Health Poverty Action. This year the event took place on 10th February; we had hero's masks and went on a hero's walk for Health Poverty Action.

Our school went through a SIAMS inspection on 3rd March in which the effectiveness of our school's Christian education and collective worship was inspected under section 48 of the Education Act 2005. This is a Statutory Inspection of Anglican and Methodist Schools (SIAMS) and is conducted in addition to Ofsted inspections for religious schools. The outcome was excellent and ECS was rated as outstanding in all the aspects of the inspection.

> The inspector wrote:
>
> *The distinctiveness and effectiveness of Emmanuel Community School as a free school with a Christian foundation are outstanding.*
>
> *The effectiveness of the religious education is outstanding.*
>
> *Emmanuel Community School is an outstanding Christian School!*
>
> *The effectiveness of the leadership and management of the school as a church school is outstanding.*

The full report of the inspection was put on our school website.

Our school kitchen was also inspected by the Food Standards Agency (FSA) the next day, and we got a 5-star rating!

The first ECS gymnastics team, comprising of Enoch, Isabelle, Jia Ming and Jia Yi, represented the school in the key stage 1 Gymnastics competition at Leyton Sixth form on the 30th of March and won a bronze medal.

We ended the term on a high with a range of Easter activities.

SUMMER TERM 2017

At the start of the summer term, we spent time in the prayer space praying for all the special people in our lives, representing them with models as we prayed. We also made prayer cups to show our appreciation for all the staff at our school. We made prayer journals, prayed for children around the world and bereaved families in Manchester, where tragically, there had been a bomb blast at a musical concert by American singer, songwriter and actress, Ariana Grande, which left many young fans dead and injured.

It was very exciting to welcome Watoto Children's Choir back on 26th May 2017. We had a great time as they performed energetically, and we were able to join in some of the songs we had practiced during our singing assemblies.

This year we entered the Quad Kids borough athletics competition for the first time, and we achieved a top 3 result with bronze medals! Well done to the team. Nancy, one of our grandparents, who was also our resident artist, worked with all of us during the Art week to create our first ever **ECS Art Gallery** in the prefabricated classroom (otherwise called the mobile building).

At the end of the term, we had great fun at the splendid Summer Fayre; from the Go Karts to the Smoothie bikes; after which we all went to the Olympic Park on 18th July and had a fabulous day. School finished at 3:30pm; and off we went to have a great summer.

11

6TH YEAR 2017/2018

SEPTEMBER 2017

The new academic year started on Tuesday 5th September with new faces and families. New parents and carers were invited for the coffee morning, two days later. Ms. Simpson became our Indigo class teacher.

Gardening Club started on 30th September with Indigo class planting daffodils around the school, ready for the spring. Mr. Lewis held a secondary school transfer meeting for children and parents on Friday 15th September to explain the secondary schools application process. Our Harvest Festival contributions were donated to Forest Churches Night Shelter, as in previous years.

Green class went on a trip to London Zoo, where they took part in an exciting educational workshop and learned all about life in the rainforest, nocturnal animals, and animal habitats.

Mr. Olokun and Mr. Blackman led the first ECS sport activity of the year, the Waltham Forest Schools football tournament on 6th October, and we had another Borough-wide Football Competition at the Chingford Goals.

During Diversity week, we focused on inspiring leaders and athletes. The Mayor of Waltham Forest, Councillor Yemi Osho, visited the school and inspired us with her life story. She also encouraged us to develop a healthy lifestyle.

Two people raised funds for our school by taking part in marathon races. Carlos ran the New York Marathon on 5th November 2017, in memory of Mrs. Iris Lewis (our head teacher's late mum). The funds he raised were used to purchase sports and playground equipment. Chris Reid had also run the London Marathon to raise funds for the school during the previous term on 14th May 2017. We later created the Chris Reid sensory garden with a story-telling chair in memory of Mrs. Lewis, who enjoyed telling us stories. The sports equipment consisted of two table tennis tables: one on the playground, the other outside our year 6 classroom.

The theme for Children in Need Day on Friday 17th November was "spotacular", so we had a non- uniform day wearing spotty clothing and had a coin race. We had a Winter Wonderland Christmas Bazaar on Saturday 9th December, and the final school day of the year ended with a candlelit Christmas carol service on Wednesday 20th December.

JANUARY - JULY 2018

As the spring term commenced, our School choir was invited to sing at the opening of Bunnings Warehouse in Fulbourne Road, Walthamstow. The PTFA also got involved in serving 'Sausage Sizzle' and engaged with parents and families to raise awareness about ECS within the local community. There was an unexpected treat when our students met the former ace footballer Fabrice Muamba at the event.

For the first time during a term, school was closed for a day because there was so much snow in London, and it was unsafe to move around.

We had our Easter Concert on Thursday March 27th.

There was a lot of anticipation for the royal baby which was eventually born to the Duke and Duchess of Cambridge, Prince William and his wife Kate. Their third child, a boy, was born on 23rd April and became fifth in line to the throne. In school, we had a royal baby card competition and even brought in our used baby clothes to create a clothes bank for distribution to babies who needed them within our community.

There was much excitement again in May, as the nation celebrated the royal wedding of Prince Harry and Meghan, who became the Duke and Duchess of Sussex. To celebrate, we had a non-uniform day with red, white and blue colours and a great picnic lunch on 18th May 2018, the day before the wedding.

Football is coming home! We did not miss out on the 2018 World Cup action. England reached the semi-finals for the first time since Italia 90. The match was shown in the school during the summer fayre on 7th July. Jordan Pickford, the England goalkeeper made three excellent saves to keep England's dream alive until the team was eventually defeated.

End of year activities included the Sports day, in which children competed using our class colours, on Tuesday 10th July. Red class went on a school trip to London Aquarium on Friday 13th July, and the whole school visited the Olympic Park in Stratford the following Tuesday.

12

7TH YEAR 2018-2019

SEPTEMBER 2018

Our final year as the premier class of Emmanuel Community School (now known as ECS) started on Wednesday 5th September at 8:55am. Since the school population was growing year on year, our classroom space was adapted from its previous use as the storage, reprographics, and intervention room. We became the Violet class, with a new teacher, Mrs. Vorster.

Some of the new things introduced this term included having our class sitting on benches at the back of the hall during assemblies, while other students sat on the floor with their legs folded. Those of us in the Rise and Shine club started reading and writing in small groups with teachers. Rise and Shine offered a range of after school activities including board games, gymnastics, art, cookery, Lego building, and much more, as part of the extended after school provision.

We had some new playground equipment installed, including wall panel games, new early years sandpit and two more table tennis tables: one in the main playground, and the other in the breakout area for years 5 and 6. Our new coach, Mr. Norman, from Tottenham Hotspur Foundation, started working with Orange and Yellow Classes.

The week commencing 10th September was exciting because we had great fun working with the author and illustrator of *Mrs. Blossom and Sniffy*, Rachel Sherfield, who worked with all of us on her story with exciting activities and workshops. On 28th September, Yellow class was visited by a literacy monster. He walked through the playground into the classroom. The children followed his footprints and found him hidden in a store cupboard. The creative exercise was part of the expressive writing and literacy lesson.

The week ended with a secondary school transfer meeting for parents of children in Indigo and Violet classes to prepare for secondary school. Our music teacher, Ms. Hardwick, returned from maternity leave on Monday, and on Thursday, there was a visit by a representative of the National Society for the Prevention of Cruelty to Children (NSPCC), with presentations that helped us understand the "Speak out, stay safe" message. On the same day, we said goodbye to Mrs. Grace, who left to have her second baby, and welcomed a new volunteer, Mrs. Houghton, a former head teacher at a local primary school, who started teaching us French.

School Council elections took place during lunchtime on 28th November, so a new school council was established for the academic year.

Staff updated their First Aid training and were also trained to use our very own Automated External Defibrillator (AED) by Danny Hyde from Emergency First Aid Ltd, who provided an excellent course. Defibrillators are known to increase survival rate in an emergency from 5% to 80%.

Children in Violet class also had the accredited First Aid training. We learnt how to resuscitate and assist people. Some parents were also trained, to equip them with the vital skills needed in emergency situations.

Pastor Chris Palmer, the Children's Pastor from Emmanuel Community Church International, attended our Wednesday assembly on 7th October. He introduced his intern – Jordan Benjamin, then spoke to us about justice (one of our school values). Thursday was National Poetry Day, and we wrote many poems which were read out in assembly. We also had Mrs. Lake, Deputy Headteacher at

Davenant Foundation School who spoke at our session for Year 5 and Year 6 after school on Friday. This was helpful because we were able to ask questions about how to choose secondary schools. There were CGP revision books available for us to order, in addition to the books we had and used in our afterschool Maths club with Mr. Okoh.

As part of our Diversity Week, we celebrated our vibrant, diverse and wonderful school community during the week of 12th October. We had fun with the young professionals who came in to inspire us with entertaining activities. Most of them had attended school on this site when it was St. Mary's Church of England School. They encouraged us to work hard and aim high. We sang in Swahili and English in our Wednesday assembly and enjoyed a visit from ex-professional footballer Fabrice Muamba (whom we met earlier at the opening of the Bunnings Store at Fulbourne Road). We ended the week listening to the Walthamstow High School for Girls steel band play interesting music in our playground.

As part of "The Desire to Inspire project", many of us took part in the Diversity Week assembly, where we acted out the life of Dr Maggie Aderin Pocock, who was named one of the top 10 most influential Black Britons in 2016 for her work as a space scientist. After half term, Mr. Olokun and Mr. Uddin took a group of year 1 and year 2 children to Tottenham Hotspur's world-class training facility in Enfield for an inter-school event, where they worked with a team of staff from Tottenham Hotspur Foundation all day. Several students, parents and families from our school were able to watch the Tottenham Hotspur versus Burnley Premier League fixture at the Wembley Stadium for free on Saturday, courtesy of Tottenham Hotspur Football club.

Prayer space club members performed a play during assembly called, *That's Not How You Pray*, a reminder that God hears us wherever we are, and He will listen whenever we talk to Him. The prayer space club gives us a chance to reflect at the beginning of the day and discuss and pray about some of the big issues in our community.

Ms. Joanna Yeung from Tottenham Hotspur's Percy House Heritage Project worked with Indigo class to provide materials, teach research techniques, prepare resources and plan information regarding the history and heritage of Walter Tull. Walter Daniel John Tull (28 April 1888-25 March 1918) was an English professional footballer and British Army officer who is widely considered the first African-Caribbean mixed heritage man to be commissioned as an infantry officer in the British Army[1].

They then presented a fantastic, thoughtful and compassionate assembly about this incredible football pioneer and war hero to the whole school.

On 4th December 2018, we had inspectors from Ofsted. The inspection was to determine whether our school continues to provide a good standard of education and whether safeguarding is effective.

During the Christmas season our school was very busy. Our years 4, 5 and 6 choir members sang at the Selbourne Walk shopping mall. They were one of the nine school choirs that sang at different points during the celebration, and we made an excellent contribution during our thirty-minute slot. We also joined other local school choirs at the Walthamstow Assembly Hall on Tuesday 18 December, in the evening, to participate in the Civic Carol Concert. It was great to sing to a packed Town Hall with all the local council dignitaries.

Our Christmas jumper day raised £600 for Save the Children charity. Our Christmas post boxes filled up fast,

---

1 https://www.nationalarchives.gov.uk/education/resources/walter-tull/

while the school councillors delivered all the cards to various classes efficiently. We received cards from different parts of the world, including from the Watoto Children's choir, who are based in Uganda. Indigo class prepared Christmas cards and practised carols, which they later sang at our local senior citizens' home. These older members of the community really enjoyed having us singing and celebrating the festive season with them.

Wednesday 19th December saw the juniors' (Green to Violet classes) much awaited and rehearsed Talent Show. This event was full of surprises with songs, dance and musical recitals. We were pleasantly surprised with party food – ECS style – and we had lots to share.

Yellow class and Mrs. Owen Reilly's team gave the school community a fantastic performance of the Nativity, with wonderful songs and great solos about the reason for the season on 17th December. Friday 21st December was the last Achievement assembly of the year, and our premier head boy (Sam), head girl (Nazareth), and prefects were announced during this assembly. The hall was lit by candlelight, and we sang Christmas Carols with the school choir. The staff room was also given a face lift with some Christmas dinner table decorations, using holly and season berries made by our garden club members.

Our Christmas prayer was read by our head boy to close the year: "*May the joy of the angels, the gladness of the shepherds, the worship of the wise men and the salvation and peace of Christ be yours....*"

JANUARY 2019

We returned to school after a lovely Christmas break to receive our Ofsted report after the December 4th inspection. Our headteacher shared the following message on the school website:

> *I am delighted to inform you that we have received the report of our recent Ofsted inspection.*
>
> *Section 8 inspections are short inspections of schools judged to be good at their most recent section 5 inspection and those outstanding schools that are not exempt from section 5. We received this kind of inspection, since we were graded good at our most recent previous inspection, of July 2014.*
>
> *The purpose of a short inspection is to determine whether the school continues to provide a good standard of education and whether safeguarding is effective.*

I am glad to say that our report shows that our school continues to provide a good standard of education and that safeguarding is effective.

We are delighted that this is the case because it is encouraging to our whole school community.

I would like to thank all of our stakeholders, including you, for the significant contribution made to the continuing success of our school.

I am sure that you would like to read the report, which takes the form of a three-and-a-half-page letter addressed to me as headteacher. (The fact that it is addressed to me is because of Ofsted procedure. Please know that this letter is to all of us.) It is available to download here:

Final Ofsted Report December 2018

We are heartened by our report and grateful for the next steps provided. We are excited about getting focused on these targets quickly and with passion.

We thank God for His continuing provision for our school and pray that He will sustain us as we press towards outstanding in all areas.

Kindest regards,

Peter Lewis
Headteacher

Some of the highlights of the Ofsted report to our head teacher are illustrated by the following excerpts:

> *"The school has grown to full capacity since the last inspection and now has its first Year 6 cohort. You and your team have ensured that the vision for the school has been maintained throughout the expansion. You, your leaders and governors are ambitious for the school and the pupils. You have taken strategic action to ensure that pupils get the best. This can be seen, for example, in how staffing and the curriculum are organised and managed.*
>
> *You continue to draw on the church as a resource for volunteer helpers and to support pupils' spiritual development. Parents and carers value the strong sense of community that you foster. They appreciate how the school lives up to its Christian ethos through*

staff who are 'unceasingly caring'. You provide a wide range of extracurricular activities to support parents and widen the experience and opportunities that pupils get.

Pupils continue to be taught well.

Leaders are vigilant in safeguarding the well-being of all pupils, including the most vulnerable. Arrangements for safeguarding and child protection are based on current statutory guidance. Procedures for reporting and recording concerns are detailed.

Pupils report that they are kept safe by staff who are caring, supportive and give them strategies to use when they have any worries."

Ref. Section 8 Ofsted Inspection on 4th December 2018

Our teachers and parents were very pleased with the outcome of the inspection.

This term, Violet class started after school booster sessions on Mondays, Wednesdays, Thursdays and Fridays. Booster sessions are extra lessons and support provided outside of normal classes to support pupils and reinforce progress. We also have specific interventions during the school day. These are highly specific additional activities, usually in maths and English. School interventions can take many forms, including one to one, or small groups, focusing on the needs of one or more children.

Extra-curricular clubs recommenced on 14th January 2019. We have a wide range of clubs covering Art, Puzzles, Film, Football and Reception Clubs. We also had waiting lists for clubs that were oversubscribed. This was often the case for sewing, athletics, football, gymnastics, or gardening clubs.

> A reception parent provided this comment in our parent feedback: *"My child has really enjoyed the reception club. They get a snack and learn through play. I was concerned that my child might be too tired after a long day, but they really enjoy continuing to learn and look forward to going each week. I think it is really good that the school provides something for each year. I know it is helpful to me. Because I can pick them up a bit later and they are safe and happy."*

In February, children in Red, Orange, and Yellow classes learned about the Chinese New Year celebration. Some of our parents presented an exciting cultural storytelling assembly. We also had the opportunity to attend fun-filled events in London. Yellow class learned about Judaism with Mrs. Jackson. She displayed different types of Kosher food. The children also learned about Jewish culture and celebrations for the Feast of Passover (*Pesach* in Hebrew) to commemorate the liberation of the Children of Israel, who were led out of Egypt by Moses.

We had our first Origami competition organised by Mr. Uddin, and seven winners were awarded some fantastic prizes for their vibrant, imaginative and creative designs. There were some really complicated designs.

It was great that some of us attended the Dynamic Young Voices concert at the world famous O2 Arena. We were performing alongside incredible actors and singers from West End Musicals, such as *Joseph and his Technicolor Dream Coat*, Tony Hadley from Spandau Ballet and Beau Dermott from *Britain's Got Talent*. We also danced along to routines with the Urban Underground dance group. The concert performance was the culmination of hard work and rehearsing at school with Mrs. Williams for over three months. It was a fantastic performance; a big thank you to Mrs. Williams for leading and inspiring us.

Feedback from a year 3 student states – *"I loved going to Young Voices at the O2; it was so good, we got to sing Gold and Gotta be Strong. My best bit was when all the parents had to stand up and dance. My grandma was laughing and dancing to Move it, Move it. I liked going because we met other schools and sang so many different songs. My teacher danced too. I think I will encourage more people to come to Young Voices next year. It is so much fun! I was a bit shy at first but when you start singing in front of the whole crowd, and you see all the tiny lights shining and parents clapping, it's amazing! I didn't ever think I would do something like this in my life and I did. Plus, I got the t-shirt!"*

Healthy Mind & Healthy Learning was our assembly theme for the week of 4th February. Mrs. Jackson and a group of children from Green, Blue and Indigo classes presented an informative assembly where they demonstrated different techniques and activities for keeping a healthy mind. They played games for good exercise and showed how encouraging and supportive words can also improve our health. We were reminded that what we eat and when we sleep has an impact on how we feel. There is a "worry box" in the hall for us to write our worries, and members of staff would contact us if we need to speak to an adult about our worries.

On 8th February, Green class went on a trip to the Natural History Museum in London. All the children listened carefully, asked interesting questions, and completed work booklets and research tasks, using the exhibits, interactive games and the famous earthquake simulator. During the trip, the class explored how the powers of volcanoes and earthquakes shape the world we live in.

In Skipping club, we made sporty, "healthy me" posters. We were given our skipping goals, which included learning Double Dutch, partners skipping, figure eight and ball schools. (Double Dutch is a jumping game played with two skipping ropes swung in opposite directions so that they cross rhythmically).

Blue Class visited the British Museum the week before half term. They studied and explored the Egyptian mummy exhibits, using their findings to complete research tasks throughout the day in small groups. They listened well, co-operated with their team members, noted key observations and asked interesting questions about the exhibits.

On the 1st of March, we had a very informative assembly about the importance of girls' education, presented by a group of girls in our school. We also received the results of our allocated secondary schools that same day.

World Book Day was colourful, exciting, and informative. Ms. Tozer led exciting story telling sessions in each class, and we all came in bright costumes depicting a book character. ECS celebrated a love of books and sharing stories during which every classroom was filled with many exciting costumes inspired by a variety of stories. This year, we have been going through the Bible, the most famous book in the world, and some of us chose to dress up as a Bible character for World Book Day. We did not recognise Mrs. Jackson, who came as Lydia in her purple outfit. There were some Old Testament characters, and indeed, a risen Jesus, among the wonderful characters.

The day started with a fun filled assembly, including an interactive performance by Ms. Tozer and a celebration of the 66 books in the Holy Bible.

We ended the week with an assembly focused on International Women's Day, to celebrate the huge contribution that women make to the nations of the world; followed by a brilliant Book swap event and tasty refreshments organized by the School Council. Over 400 books were donated and over 200 were swapped. Blue Class donated over 100 books and won the Biggest Book Swap donation class prize!

> We often have visitors at our school, one visitor provided the following feedback after being shown around while classes were going on:

> *"Thank you for my visit, this is a welcoming school with a professional atmosphere and happy children. I enjoyed visiting the school and looking at the quality of work displayed around the school. I can see all the children work very hard. I hope to be invited back soon."*
>
> Anon. visitor

We received a certificate and a Thank You note for the £125 we raised for the Poppy Appeal. The certificate was displayed in the school office reception. The citation read: "*Without your help we would be unable to continue our vital welfare and benevolent work*", signed by Mr. McMillian, the Local Honorary Organiser. The Poppy Appeal is the **Royal British Legion's** biggest fundraising campaign held every year in November, during the period of Remembrance.

Red Class had a very exciting week as they marked Ash Wednesday with traditional pancakes in the classroom. They counted and measured the right ingredients, then carefully watched the mixture change texture from a liquid to a solid form. They all dressed in colourful costumes for World Book Day, followed by a parent reader session.

They visited the Walthamstow library earlier in the week, so they had lots of books to take home to read.

SUMMER TERM 2019

After Easter, there was a lot to concentrate on as we prepared for our Standard Assessment Tests. Commonly referred to as SATS, these are National Curriculum tests conducted across the country, and which enables comparison and benchmarking of performance. Mr Ben Okoh ran mathematics classes after school on Fridays and he always made the subject interesting.

As the first set of year 6 children at ECS, there was a lot of excitement about completing our primary education. After some consultation between staff and the Parents Teachers and Friends association, it was decided that bespoke graduation gowns would be sewn for the imminent graduation ceremony.

In the meantime, once the SATS were out of the way and results were awaited, we had the opportunity to do more extra-curricular activities. These included First Aid training (which has since become a yearly tradition for subsequent sets of Year 6 students).

We went on a residential trip to Gilwell Park for a few days of adventure and fun. Gilwell Park is a camp site and activity centre located in Sewardstone, Essex, which is in

Epping Forest and close to Chingford, London. The 109-acre site is owned by The Scout Association. We really enjoyed the activities and had lots of fun.

We received our SATS exam results and the outcomes for maths and spelling, punctuation and grammar (SPAG) were fantastic. A thanksgiving/graduation service was held at our partner church Emmanuel Community Church International in July 2019 to mark the end of the school year, which included presentations of new Bibles to each year 6 student.

13

LOOK HOW FAR WE HAVE COME

The first cohort of students concluded their time at ECS in July 2019. Below is a reflection from our Head teacher Mr Peter Lewis:

I wrote the following in our yearbook of 2013, at the end of our school's first ever academic year on our permanent site:

> *I will never forget the day that Emmanuel Community School opened. I remember standing at the entrance to the school, watching our children walking along the street wearing their pristine new uniforms and thinking how amazing it was to see that a brand-new school had opened.*

What was true then is true now, and I still remember the first day of our school with a level of immense gratitude and humility.

The psalmist, in Psalm 77 verse 11, states: *I will remember the deeds of the Lord....*(NIV)

I surely do remember the Lord's deeds. Indeed, it was the Lord who provided the vision for our school, caused and enabled it to open, and He has been with us every step of the way. We thank and praise Him.

Now we are at a point where our first ever children are about to leave for secondary school. It is amazing to consider how far the Lord has brought us. Our school is now a thriving, complete primary school with classes ranging the whole primary phase: Reception to Year 6. God is good.

As I reflect on this awesome moment, I would like to highlight a few things:

- The voice of the Lord is powerful (Psalm 29 verse 4). It is the Lord who spoke our school into being and it is the Lord who sustains it.
- Our "outstanding in all areas" SIAMs inspection (Statutory Inspection of Anglican and Methodist Schools) which stated: '*The school has a very strong and clear Christian foundation which*

directly and positively expresses its service to its diverse community'.

- Comments from our two Ofsted inspections: '*Teaching is good, because staff have high expectations…Outstanding leadership by the headteacher, leaders and governors has established a good school… Parents and carers value the strong sense of community. They appreciate how the school lives up to its Christian ethos through staff who are 'unceasingly caring'.*

We have an amazing school community: Titilayo Oluwatudimu, the school's founder and Director of Education; The Emmanuel School Trust; the governing body; staff; PTFA; parents and carers; the children and many others. Without everyone 'rowing together' it would be hard to move forward, so we look to keep working as a team to see where the journey next takes us.

One thing, for sure, is that we can depend upon the Lord. A beautiful cake was made for the school's opening ceremony. The writing on it quoted Jeremiah chapter 29 verse 11. Here is that verse in full:

> *"For I know the plans I have for you," declares the Lord, "plans to prosper you and not to harm you, plans to give you hope and a future." (NIV)*

Let us thank God for all that he has done to bring us this far. Let us abide in the goodness of God as we move forward.

Peter Lewis,

Headteacher 2012 -2022

PART THREE

INDIVIDUAL REFLECTIONS OF OUR TIME AT ECS

(FROM 1ST COHORT YEAR 6 CLASS OF 2019)

In the concluding section below, some of our children reflect on their years at Emmanuel Community School.

14

CHILD ONE

I joined Emmanuel Community School five years ago at the age of 6, and I still vividly remember walking in the first time, in year 1. Ever since, I have been in this school preparing for my SATS.

On my first day, slowly walking into Emmanuel was really frightening. My parents were beside me and gave me a warm smile before they left. Eventually, when I went in, I was really shy since I didn't know anyone in the room. When it was break time, I made friends who are still my friends to this day. A few days later, two more girls came, and I remember crying because I wasn't the new girl anymore. It was really embarrassing (everyone staring, and the teacher was laughing). Now thinking about it, it was quite hilarious. Near the end of year 1, our teacher left the school, and we got a new teacher. I thought she was a terrible teacher.

Going into year 2, I thought she was going to be the worst, but she ended up being a marvellous and amazing teacher. She really helped me and encouraged me to do my best. When we had science week, I had about 10 time-outs in one day for bad behaviour, but apart from that I was an angel. I also met my best friend, and she has been by my side ever since.

Going into year 4, I was really excited and made a new friend. I was also ecstatic to get a new teacher. My new teacher was extremely tall. He was really funny, and made impressions of teachers in our school, but when he got angry, he would really shout. All in all, he was fantastic!

Year 5 was my best year. I had the best teacher. Since I loved to draw, I was hit by inspiration when we did art in class. I always tried my best and worked hard. Throughout my years, I have always got a good report and have had high scores.

During year 5, I went to summer camp, run by the church from our school, and it was amazing. In my room were two of my best friends and another child I knew very well, even though she was younger than me. We had so much fun. We did axe throwing, hiking and even mountain rolling. We also had midnight snacks and brought lots of food. We always slept late, and we were the noisiest group. For lunch we had delicious foods like pasta, and for dinner, hot chocolate. There were so many activities like zip lining, football and canoeing.

In year 6, I was working towards my SATS and trying to achieve the best results. We did extra learning after school, and we planned to go on an end of year trip to the same camp.

I appreciate all the encouragement given to me. If I were to stay in one school, it would be this one. I am really excited for year 7 and I am hoping to do my best.

15

CHILD TWO

Looking back at my time at Emmanuel Community School, it has been a crazy adventure. I was 5 when I came to this school in 2012. Now it is 2019, 7 years on. I came here so I could learn, but I haven't only learnt about subjects and how to be competent, I have learnt how to be a good person. This is how it began:

My first day was a bit tough. I was weary and wouldn't walk, as I stepped in, my mum accompanied me upstairs. My teacher welcomed me with a smile and said, "Good morning, welcome to ECS, I will be your teacher". After 10 minutes, my mum left and my best friend arrived. (I knew her because she lived next door to me). I would not talk to anyone except one of the adults. A few weeks later, I became more sociable.

My first lesson was Maths, and I was so confused, as was everyone else, because it was the first time we did real Maths.

Our school used to be on Erskine Road, but after reception we moved to bigger buildings on The Drive. In year one, we got a new teacher, and a new student joined. A few weeks later, another student joined, and they became best friends, because they were both Spanish. Later, another student arrived. As soon as it was break, I approached her and said, "If you want to play?" From that moment on, we became best friends. Sadly, the teacher left. The Head teacher came to teach us, and we learnt a new story called *Naughty Bus*. One afternoon, I walked into the classroom and, surprisingly, our work was on display. We were astonished. The work on the wall was written by both of us. A few months later, we had our 6.5 weeks holiday.

Year 2 was amazing because I learned to join up my handwriting! I learnt how to use the column method, and I could write legibly! Also, we got a new teacher. Then a new girl joined, and we became friends. Another boy joined too. I had a fun year.

In year 3, we got a new teacher, who later got married. I wrote my first three-page story. We started to learn our times tables. I struggled a little bit and was scared that I would get everything wrong because the work was much harder.

Year 4 was one of my favourite years. I made so many friends and I had a great teacher. He was my favourite, but he left when I was in year 5. A new student arrived, and we all became friends with her. The year was great! Unfortunately, that was the year one of my best friends left and everyone cried!

Year 5 was also one of my favourite years, because we had a teacher that I was very familiar with. Even though it was one of my favourite years, it was a tough year. We had to learn our times tables off by heart, we did loads of difficult tests, and we also had the great opportunity of writing about one of my favourite stories.

Year 6 was amazing, but also scary! The start of the year was good. A new student joined our class. It was also SATS year, and it got much harder. We had loads more tests and booster classes after school. We had been writing about loads of topics and doing lots of work to prepare for SATS.

I have had a great time at ECS, but I look forward to secondary school. I am going to miss my friends terribly. What will I do without them? They are always going to be my friends. If I were you, I would come to this school, so you can experience a great education too.

16

CHILD THREE

In 2012 a breath-taking new school (called Emmanuel Community School) opened in Erskine Road. This school was part church too. My time at ECS so far has been memorable and I would like to share some of my exciting moments so far.

As I hopped down the road (on my first day of school) my mum and dad accompanied me by holding each of my hands (and no, I'm not an alien, they held one hand each). When I strolled into the vast classroom, I paused. My parents said "Bye", as they convinced me that I would be fine. I listened to them, and, in a quiet voice, I whispered "Hi," to my new teacher.

After a few weeks it was World Book Day. I posed in my front yard as my mum took a picture of me wearing a bright pink dress with sequins. At the end of this year, I realised that school was not bad.

"Hello, year 5, I am your teacher!" An amiable, tall woman said. As everyone jumped up and shouted "Yay!" our new teacher came into the room. We were all happy, because in 2014 she came on a trip with us, then left, and then she was back in 2017. This year was one of my favourite years because we got to make and eat sherbet and muffins in science.

During year 6 we are being helped by our teacher to make amelioration on our grammar and arithmetic skills. At the start of year 6, I felt a little bit uneasy that I wouldn't know what to do or how I would cope, but my teacher helped me. In this year, my class and I learnt a new game called 'Rotten Egg'. It is where someone runs around the circle and drops a bit of tissue behind a person. Now that we are 6 months in, I've perceived that this year is guiding us to a better future.

In just four weeks we will be doing our SATS and then some children will be going camping. I also can't wait for secondary school and all the other trips that we will be going on. So, if I were you, I would be excited too.

17

CHILD FOUR

Hi, I'm writing/recounting my life at Emmanuel Community School because I'm leaving very soon. Maybe we can start off at Erskine Road, at the time where most kids start school.

MY FIRST DAY AT SCHOOL

To me, that day wasn't an ordinary day, but most definitely extraordinary; a day where most kids were nervous about leaving nursery. Sure, I had a queasy stomach, but I was extremely excited. New school, new clothes and a totally new beginning, sweet! I don't remember much, but I do remember Mr. Lewis (our head teacher) saying he was proud to have so many children start a new school. Unfortunately, we weren't there for the whole day. Gradually, we got to stay at school for longer. Anyway, time to move on....

MY TWO MOST EMBARRASSING MOMENTS

Let's make this quick, so I can forget about this. So, in reception, my favourite staff member tickled me so hard that I peed on myself.... The second most embarrassing thing that has happened to me was one afternoon when I said something silly to one of my friends and he chased me across the whole playground. When I finally thought I had gotten away, and went to get some water, I got smacked on the back by him which caused me to pee—once again. To be fair, he hit me hard.

MY PREFERRED SUBJECTS

Hmm, that's a tough one since I like most of my lessons, but maybe I should write down 5: History, ICT, Maths, Literacy, and Science. Most of the time, they are very interesting. For example, in literacy on 11th March, we wrote a formal letter, in Maths on 25th March, we worked on ratio, etc., etc. I ought to talk about the others, but I will not.

YEAR 6 SO FAR

It wasn't so good in the beginning, because I always got on the teacher's nerves and then in very big trouble. Now I'm fine; in fact, I'm getting on as smooth as a pebble. But very soon (so soon that it's in a few days), I and other kids in different schools will be doing SATs, so I need to work hard. Some people (who are my friends) in year 7 told me SATs is a joke, but I don't believe them... or do I? May I continue?

HOPES AND DREAMS

Ah, it looks like I've reached the end of my recount, so I guess it's time for my hopes and dreams and how I feel about leaving primary. I'm looking forward to going to my secondary school, since they do everything I'm hoping and dreaming to do. Professional basketball, science, sports and advanced Maths, and don't forget Christianity. Of course, I'll miss Emmanuel Community School (after all I've been here for 7 years), but this is life, you must move on. Anyway, I've reached the end of my recount, so I guess this is goodbye. I will be in my secondary academy learning to code in the coding club, and I'll also get to do experiments in science.

18

CHILD FIVE

Hello, my name is *xxx*. I'm going to secondary school next year. My mum hasn't told me where I am going yet, but I want to go to Davenant.

In reception, I went to Romania and came back in year 2. In year 2, on the first day, the teacher presented me to the class, but everyone knew me already.

In year 3, there was a play with me as one of the angels. I didn't really say anything, just to sing lots of songs. Then I went to Romania.

In year 5, when I came back from Romania, we did a class assembly.

In year 6, we are planning a concert and we are writing, and I see this as very good.

In future I want to be a professional basket baller.

19

CHILD SIX

The first day of Emmanuel Community School for me was in November. The reason I moved to Emmanuel Community School was because I moved houses. So now I will tell you about my life in school so far.

Eight o'clock, I walked nervously into the hall. The reason I wasn't going into the classroom was because I went to breakfast club. The first person I met made me feel very welcome. Then an hour later, I went into the playground to meet all the other people. One of my first friends was being lazy, but she was fun to play with.

At the end of the school year, there was a summer camp. So, my mum paid for me to go. Many people who I knew went, including my best friend and some boys in my class. Three people I knew were in my dorm with me. My favourite activity was probably laser tag. At summer camp we created history! On the last day of summer camp, I was excited to see my family but sad because it was still ages until I could see my friends again.

In Year 5, my teacher always made everything fun and made us laugh. My favourite subject in year 5 was P.E. The last day of the year ended with a party and, when our teacher put on a song, we all would dance or sing along.

I went to summer camp again. All the same people came but another friend came this time. My favourite activity was axe throwing. The people who were in my dorm included a girl who left Emmanuel Community School and me. We did nearly the exact same things as before, but other fun stuff too. By the end of summer camp, I felt the same but felt sadder that I had to leave two of my best friends forever (BFF).

The beginning of year 6 was fun, but then the work got harder. Even though the work got harder, I still enjoyed it. My favourite piece of English was our blackout poetry[2]. A part of mine went like this:

"Another sun glistening
wild dogs running
this is Africa, dung beetles abound.
This vast dusty continent mist,

---

[2] Blackout poetry is when you take a written piece of text from a book, newspaper, or magazine and redact words, in order to come up with your own story.

the savanna as mountain streams.
Leopard print fresh in the sand,
my heart beats louder
this is Eden ultimate wonderland".

So, as you can probably tell we are being taught a lot of information by our teacher. My favourite subject is P.E. Our teacher is from South Africa, so, she has taught us different games that most people in London have never heard of. My favourite game (that we have been taught) is *Rotten Egg*.

Even though I didn't start this school in reception, I have listed all the years I've been in so far. In a couple of months, me and all my class members are going to secondary school. The school I'm going to is Walthamstow Girls Academy. Three other people (who are in my class) are going there too. I will miss everyone else, but I will still have contact with some people.

So that is all my life at Emmanuel Community. I hope you enjoyed it! I think I will enjoy high school and have a job as a designer.

20

EPILOGUE

GOING FORWARD

It is imperative that the Trust continues the journey to consolidate Emmanuel Community School as a successful and sustainable long-term initiative. The Trust's bid to the DfE in 2011 was highly commended for its education vision and innovative concepts. The task of implementing the vision and bringing the concepts to fruition required utmost dedication.

In addition to establishing and embedding good practice and excellence at Emmanuel Community School, the Trust aspires to collaborate with stakeholders and other organisations to further influence educational provision.

In the process of casting a vision for the school around 2010, we consulted those who ultimately matter most (children). The feedback was very revealing. For example, one youngster's wish list for their school is as follows:

- An artistic curriculum, so every lesson is exciting, artistic and fun
- Adults that care, who are not just teaching as a profession
- Lots of motivational speakers coming in
- Opportunities to be 'scouted' for things they are good at
- Lots of competitions to prove their skills
- A good sports programme involving other schools
- Mentors coming in to speak to some children
- If there's a problem, it should be sorted immediately and fairly
- Trusted staff members, so children can tell them anything and be confident they won't tell others unless it is necessary.

TIMELINE

Here is a summary of the key milestones in the journey to establishing this school:

- *Spring 2010 - Lead Proposer elaborates the Vision, following challenge from Ministers. Meets with Pastors, Elders and Trustees of Emmanuel*

Christian Centre, offering the proposal as an ECC/G&T initiative. Proposal is endorsed.

- *Spring 2010 – Recruiting initial team of volunteers and testing out ideas on focus groups.*
- *Spring - Winter 2010 – extensive consultations with New Schools Network (NSN). Team members attend conferences, workshops and familiarize themselves with emerging policies and processes for setting up free schools.*
- *Pro-bono support sought from specialist consultants and Free School proponents.*
- *Autumn 2010 – Initial application and bid documentation are submitted to DfE for selection to be part of the first tranche of Free schools. Greenleaf Trust, an existing charity is proposed as the Academy Trust.*
- *Winter 2010 – DfE changes criteria and protocol for applications, nullifying the application. It's back to the drawing board.*
- *Spring 2011 - Lead proposer and key collaborators re-write the Bid against a very tight deadline, culminating in a document setting out the vision, ethos and sustainability criteria for the school.*

  - *Bid requires detailed research into demography, social characteristics and educational attainment of catchment area to clarify whether there's a clear need for a new school.*
  - *Parallel discussions undertaken to establish size of school, proposed name and logo, alongside intense efforts to identify suitable sites within the selected catchment area.*
  - *Meetings held with Waltham Forest LEA officials, councillors, and portfolio holder for Education and Young People, leader of Council, local MP, business leaders, and other stakeholders.*
  - *Public consultations undertaken, and names, post codes and addresses of prospective students drawn up as evidence of need.*
- *May 2011 - The Emmanuel School Trust (TEST) is Incorporated.*
- *May 2011 - THE BID is submitted to the DfE with much prayer.*
- *July 2011 – DfE announces shortlist of bids selected for next stage of application. ECS is on the*

shortlist and the TEST team is invited for a formal interview.

- *September 2011 – 7 members of team attend interview at DfE offices at Westminster, London (near Houses of Parliament).*
- *October 2011 – VICTORY! The letter arrives from the Secretary of State for Education - our bid has been approved to go to pre-opening stage. The baby has been born!*
- *Winter 2011 - Search for school site intensifies. Advert placed for Head Teacher.*
- *December 2011 - Interviews for Head Teacher.*
- *January 2012 - Project Managers, Marketing and Educational consultants appointed from DfE framework, following evaluation of competitive bids.*
- *February 2012 – Emmanuel Christian Centre Trustees agree to proposal for TEST to share their premises at Erskine Road as temporary site for one year.*
- *April 2012 - Head Teacher – Mr. Peter Lewis starts.*
- *May 2012 – Formal Public Consultation with Stakeholders. (NUT branch opposed to*

Government's free school policy pickets a parent evening held on Greenleaf Road!)

Head Teacher, Trustees, Pastors, Members of ECC all work hard to publicise the fact that our new school will be opening, despite uncertainty about its permanent site.

- *May 2012 - Start advertising for staff*
- *June 2012 - Readiness to Open review – Is Project Emmanuel RED or GREEN? (Make or break meeting at Department for Education).*
- *July 2012 - Building work starts on temporary site.*
- *July 2012 - Readiness to Open meeting at Department for Education.*
- *July 2012 - Pre-opening OFSTED inspection. Temporary premises is given the green light.*
- *July 2012 - Resources purchased, staff employed, but the all-important Funding Agreement is not signed yet!*
- *11th August 2012 - Funding Agreement signed – Hallelujah!*
- *3rd September 2012 - Staff start work.*
- *6th September 2012 - Emmanuel Community School Opens!*

- *10th September 2012 - First cohort of students start school.*
- *September 2013 – School opens on permanent site on The Drive.*
- *July 2014 - 1st OFSTED inspection.*
- *3rd March 2017 - SIAMS inspection.*
- *4th December 2018 - 2nd OFSTED inspection.*
- *July 2019 – Graduation of the first cohort of students.*

AUTHOR'S BIOGRAPHY

Titilayo was born and raised in Nigeria. She settled in Great Britain thirty years ago after six years in Italy. Teaching, for her, is more of a calling than a career as she passionately seeks to equip young people to turn life's barriers into stepping stones.

The late Revd Dr Joel Edwards CBE, ex- General Director of the UK Evangelical Alliance, was emphatic that Christians should be proactive in their faith and live out scriptural principles in every sphere of life. Titilayo has a similar unwavering conviction that, since Jesus Christ demonstrated that children are special, Christian organisations have a responsibility to their communities in the provision of childcare facilities and education.

Although her specialism is Mathematics and Science at secondary level, Titilayo has co-ordinated the vision and implementation of several primary education initiatives. Apart from her work in schools, she has been keenly involved in youthwork, serving as the Vice Chair of the former African Caribbean Evangelical Alliance's Children and Youth (CandY) ministry. She has also led activity camps as National Youth Coordinator for the Overseas Fellowship of Nigerian Christians (OFNC). Titilayo was a founding Director of the Greenleaf Trust, a charity focused on local community initiatives aimed at children, youth and adults.

Titilayo was the Lead Proposer of Emmanuel Community School and is currently Chief Executive Officer of The Emmanuel School Trust.

Printed in Great Britain
by Amazon

37365850R00106